MY *Father*
DOESN'T OWN A
GAS STATION

DICK BERNAL

Scripture quotations are from the New King James Version of The Holy
Bible, copyright 1991 by Thomas Nelson, Inc., and The Message - The
New Testament In Contemporary Language, NavPress Publishing Group,
1993. Used by permission.

ISBN 1-884920-21-7

(Originally published, *Diary of a Reluctant Recruit* © 1988
ISBN 0-88144-127-9)

(Thereafter published as, *Kingdom Journey* © 1996
ISBN 1-884920-06-3)

PUBLISHED BY
Jubilee Christian Center
175 Nortech Parkway
San Jose, California 95134
www.jubilee.org

PRINTED IN THE UNITED STATES OF AMERICA

TABLE OF CONTENTS

FOREWORD

Pastor Dick is a man who is willing to courageously do God's will at the cost of friendships, reputation, or social opinion. Having been in his employ for nearly ten years I interacted closely with him. I stood with him in hard times, in the stress of building programs, negative press, family problems, and unethical behavior of trusted church personnel. He always managed to make it to the next round and keep on fighting.

Pastor Dick is man enough to admit when he is wrong, sensitive enough to share grief, and quick to help those in need. He is bold enough to confront foolishness, willing to give you the shirt off his back, always prepared to tell a funny story, and trusting in the face of great risk.

Proverbs tells us that a people without a vision will perish. Pastors Dick and Carla are visionaries. Through years of obstacles I've watched them plant and replant the vision for Jubilee Christian Center. There have been many who have tried to discredit their methods and motives; but by the Holy Spirit's power they have held steady with a vision of bringing the kingdom of God to local folks and spreading the gospel worldwide.

As you read Dick's life story you will laugh, cry, rejoice, and experience the passion of a man who was a reluctant recruit in the army of the Lord. In spite of his admitted weaknesses and shortcomings, Dick has become one of the leading authorities on spiritual warfare and church growth.

I am convinced in my heart that because of Dick and Carla's pastoral love, counsel, and friendship, my ministry in the Lord has been blessed and enhanced. I will always love and appreciate them. They hold a very special place in my heart.

Ron Kenoly

International Worship Leader

October 30, 1944 ~ October 30, 2004

My first 60 years was quite a ride ...

Can't wait to experience the next 60 years!

PART ONE

ENTERING THE KINGDOM

"The time is fulfilled,

and the kingdom of God is at hand.

Repent, and believe in the gospel."

-Mark 1:15

INTRODUCTION

I was invited by a friend to Bogotá, Colombia in January of 2001 to attend an annual World G-12 Conference hosted by Pastor Cesar Castellanos and the International Charismatic Mission (ICM). I had previously met Cesar and Claudia Castellanos at a conference in Baker, Louisiana prior to coming to Bogotá. I was astonished by their zeal for the Gospel even after an assassination attempt on both their lives that left Cesar plugged with 5 bullet holes and Claudia shot with one.

I was now a bit eager to see firsthand the phenomenal revival this church and city were experiencing, hoping that some of what they had might rub off on me, Jubilee, and our city, San Jose, California. ICM has truly made an impact in Bogotá. While there I met presidential candidate, Alvaro Uribe Velez, who was attending the conference, not only because he wanted prayer for the upcoming election, but because he was also involved in ICM's cell life. I also learned that there were several other government officials involved in ICM's church – one Senator Jose and his wife Clarita Villanueva who were pastoring 5,000 cells throughout the city. When a church has this much influence on its city, they are a force for good!

After participating in a full day of meetings and other activities, I retired to my hotel room for the evening, exhausted. As I lay there in a daze reflecting on the incredible things I was taking in, I began to imagine the possibilities that could take place in my own backyard. I was so keyed up not being able to sleep that I switched the television on only to find a local newscast reporting a devastating earthquake that shook India that day. The shaker measured 7.9 on the Richter scale.

I must do something, was my first thought. I wanted to raise some money for humanitarian relief. You will see why India wasn't just another country in need.

When I returned to San Jose, I called my personal friend, entertainer M.C. Hammer, who had connections with the Silicon Valley Indian community. I was informed that they had already begun organizing something but didn't have a venue to meet. I volunteered our large sanctuary and everything began coming into place.

The Indian community welcomed my offer, and in no time M.C. Hammer, Deepak Chopra and various Hindu *Bollywood* celebrities were confirmed to help in the fundraising efforts.

A missionary at heart, I viewed this as a humanitarian effort on my part, nothing more.

In a couple of weeks' time, even former President Bill Clinton declared that he too wanted to help India's earthquake victims. There's probably no better fundraiser and celebrated spokesman for a cause than former President Bill Clinton. When he found his way into my San Jose, California office my Evangelical and Republican friends were thrown into a primeval panic. They went ballistic; it's as if their brains had grasped too much in too short a time.

My philosophy was simple: Could I as a Christian pastor let politics, religion, or anything else interfere with my ability to help India's devastated earthquake victims —including its women and children?

It's just as well that God works in mysterious ways.

If I had known all the anxiety and unrest associated with preaching the kingdom of God in word, deed, and in power, it would have been too much for me. After all, here, I was simply demonstrating brotherly love - things pertaining to the kingdom of God - to my hurting East India neighbors a world away.

My spiritual autobiography is about that kingdom, the kingdom of God on earth.

CHAPTER 1

WHO IS GOD?

I grew up in Watsonville, a sleepy agricultural town in Northern California. My parents divorced before I was two-years-old, but I received plenty of love and security from my mother, two older sisters, and wonderful grandparents. Because my mother worked six days a week from sun up to sun down, my grandmother played a major role in shaping my young life.

My Uncle Dick drowned in 1941 while saving a woman's life in a flash flood. When I was born three years later, my mom named me after him, I think to help fill a void left by his death. Uncle Dick had been posthumously awarded the Wellman's medal of honor for sacrificing his life for another. As a boy I wore this bronze medal on a chain around my neck. Today the medal is a tender reminder of God's call on my life spending it in the service of others. But, I'm getting ahead of myself.

In spite of death and divorce in our extended family, ours was not a sad house. In fact, there was lots of laughter. Grandma had a kind of innocent humor that kept me in stitches. Once the *L.A. Dodgers* were playing the *San Francisco Giants* on television. Sandy Koufax was ripping in the fastballs and striking out player after player. Grandma sat on the edge of the sofa, squinting at the television. Finally, she said, "That Sandy fellow isn't very nice. He's throwing the ball so fast that those poor boys can't hit it!"

My sisters, Judy and Juanita, became two of my closest friends. I'd be curious and wide-eyed as they would drag me around town.

My first day of kindergarten was in September 1949. I could hardly sleep the night before. *Oh boy,* I thought. *Now I can go along with my two big sisters to Freedom Elementary School!* My kindergarten teacher would be Miss Tyman, who had taught both Judy and Juanita.

The next morning Grandma took me by the hand and led me into what seemed a cavernous room. Thirty-three little desks were neatly lined up with name tags in place. Grandma carefully looked for Dickie Bernal's name.

"There it is Dickie!" she exclaimed, pointing to one near the back.

I sat down and my friend Gary Goldman plopped down next to me. We grinned at each other. Gary was a strange looking kid. He had a shock of white hair that stood straight up. No amount of butch wax could tame that mop.

Miss Tyman began the day by suggesting that each of us stand, one by one, and tell our new classmates what our fathers did for a living. I panicked and found it hard to breathe. Daddy? My father was a stranger to me. He was a big dark-haired handsome fellow, but I had no idea what he did. Oh, he'd show up every few months with a toy or a new dollar for us kids. Then he'd make Momma cry. I didn't have a clue about how to relate to him.

One by one the kids stood up, ever so proud to announce their fathers' vocations. It was Gary's turn. Gary popped up, stuck out his chest, looked around the room and declared, "My father owns a gas station."

My turn came. Miss Tyman asked, "Dickie, what does your father do for a living?" I wanted to run home. Slowly, I rose to my feet. I glanced at Grandma out of the corner of my eye. She gave me one of those looks only Grandma could give: "Honey boy, I love you but lie and you die!"

I looked back at Miss Tyman and took a deep breath. Squirming like a rabbit caught in a trap, I whispered, "My father owns a gas station too." Then I sat down as fast as humanly possible. It seemed like an eternity before I mustered the courage to look Grandma's way. Her expression was unmistakable: "I'll see you later, Sonny boy."

I'm dead meat, I thought.

Walking home that day I kicked every rock, cigarette butt, and soda can. I walked into the house and was greeted with a command. "Go get me a switch, young man."

"Okay Grandma," I answered, trying to act brave. I had been through the ritual before. Grandma was small but had a swing on her like Babe Ruth. I gave her my hand-picked instrument of punishment. She turned it over in her hands, making sure it passed the spanking specs. It did. Telling me to bend over, she said, "Shame on you, Dickie! Never lie no matter what."

Grandma, I'd rather take a beating any day than feel shame again, I thought to myself. At four years and eleven months of age, I figured that lying was better than feeling embarrassed.

All we like sheep have gone astray; we have turned, every one, to his own way. ~ISAIAH 53:6

✎ My Early Years

During my grade school years in Watsonville, my friends were Japanese, Mexican, and Jewish. I didn't think that this was unusual until other kids made racial remarks that seemed mean to me. One of my Japanese friends taught me how to count to ten in Japanese. I remember feeling sorry for my Mexican friend Tommy whose bedroom had cracks clear through it, but envied him for his warm and loving Dad and Mom.

I loved Saturday afternoon matinees, especially the adventure movies set in mysterious places like India or Africa. Movies like *Gunga Din* and *Sabu*, the jungle boy. Cobras and tigers fascinated me.

But the biggest thing that happened in those years was television! "Can you believe it?" I asked Tommy when we saw the black and white picture on the screen for the first time. "It's like having your own movie theater at home!"

A rich kid in our neighborhood lived in a two-story house. His parents had a gardener, a new station wagon with wood-like paneling, and best of all, a television set. I never really liked that boy until his dad bought the television. Then he quickly became the most popular boy on our block. We spent a lot of time at his house, especially after school when *Howdy Doody* came on.

Uncle Bob, Milton Berle, Ed Sullivan, and of course, the Lone Ranger, all became my weekly friends. Before long we owned a television of our own. No longer did I play kick-the-can or hide-and-go-seek until dark. In retrospect, I believe it was healthier playing our favorite games. But at the time we called it progress.

There were not a lot of programs on Saturday afternoons that we watched, except for a very different kind of telecast that came on at about 4:00 p.m. The telecast was from an enormous tent packed with thousands of people, and featured a preacher from Oklahoma named Oral Roberts. This man preached like a house on fire about the wages of sin, and how only God's grace and mercy could save people from eternal damnation.

Then he would do something most unusual. He would sit on a chair, lay his hand on the head of each person in a long line, and yell, "Be healed!"

When he did this his head would jerk and his hair would fly around. Sweat poured down his face. Even to many people who were faithful churchgoers, his program was a real wild scene. The entire scenario captivated us. Once in awhile, one of the grown-ups in the room would remark, "Do you suppose this is all real?" None of us dared say it was a fake for fear of God's wrath, so we just sat there wondering in silence. Not being churchgoing folks, we had no idea what was real and what was not.

The whole God-and-Jesus thing became a little confusing for me. Often Grandma read her Bible late at night. She obviously revered the Word of God, although she never commented on it. But she sure believed in honesty, clean living, and the respect of children for their elders.

Grandma really enjoyed a religious program by Bishop Fulton Sheen. I would watch this oddly dressed man with piercing eyes and a reassuring voice. He spoke of God's goodness and love.

One Saturday afternoon, a couple of us guys snuck into a big Roman Catholic Church on Main Street to check things out.

After daring one another, we tiptoed through the door and took a look. The big gothic edifice sent chills up my spine. It reminded me of a movie I once saw about a deformed man, *The Hunchback of Notre Dame*. To make things even spookier, there was a school next door named Notre Dame.

We inched ourselves down the aisle. There were candles lit up toward the front of the church. The flickering glow charged the atmosphere with mystery. We made it down to a rail, where I stared up at a poor, tormented individual hanging on a huge cross. His eyes were looking upward as if crying out for help from some invisible force. His face, hands, and feet had blood on them. We had begun inching backwards toward the door, when suddenly the sound of footsteps from behind a side curtain startled me.

"Run for it!" I yelled.

We hit the front door running and didn't stop until we passed the graveyard on Freedom Boulevard. Then we all laughed like crazy, figuring we had tempted fate and gotten out alive. Oddly enough, we never talked about that day again. Yet the images I had encountered, especially the man on the cross, remained with me for a long time. I remember lying on my bed thinking how lonely the man looked.

Why did they hang him on a cross? I asked myself. *What did he do to deserve such a horrible death?*

At the other end of the religious spectrum was the little storefront Pentecostal Holiness church down near the Pajaro River, next door to the Center Theater. When my ten-year-old buddies and I stood in line for the Sunday morning matinee, we'd hear the folks inside the little church shouting, whooping, and hollering. It seemed as though you could hear them for a mile. When we came out of the movie theater, they'd still be at it. What in the world was going on in there?

One Sunday afternoon, we decided to sneak in and see for ourselves. We slipped through the front door, trying to be inconspicuous. Forty to fifty adults were jumping up and down, hands raised as if someone had a gun to their backs. Their eyes looked dazed and they were yelling all kinds of things. Some were speaking a strange foreign language I had never heard before. One big black lady was rolling around on the floor as if she was having a seizure or something. Without a word, we beat it for the door at the same time. We were scared that we'd catch whatever was wrong with them.

Every now and then a thought would pester me. *Who is God anyway?* Did God live on a cross in that scary church down on Main, or did He hang out with the weird people next to the theater? Or was God with Oral Roberts in that big tent? What about Bishop Sheen in his strange costume? Did he speak for God?

That Christmas I played the role of an extra shepherd in the school Nativity play. As I gazed down at the little doll in the manger, I wondered who Jesus was. Jesus must be a good guy, because He gets me out of school for two weeks at Christmas and another week at Easter. But I wondered why such a nice man had to die such a terrible death.

Finally, I decided that I would understand all this after I grow up. My folks surely never discussed it.

MY FIRST PRAYER

The next fall going into the sixth grade I felt big and important.

Together with my buddy David, I was asked to try out for the school's basketball team. Each year an outstanding sixth grader was asked to join the seventh and eighth graders' A or B squad. This was the big leagues! You would get to travel all the way to Salinas or even up to Hollister. Also, you could wear the blue and white colors of *Freedom Elementary Union* in front of cheering masses. Was there anything in the whole world more important than my making the team? Not for me!

My only obstacle was David. He was a good free-throw shooter, but I had a better jump shot from the floor. Plus, I was an inch taller and had all the right moves. No problem!

The night before the team members were chosen, I figured a little prayer wouldn't hurt. Maybe it would give me the extra edge. I had never prayed before because I had never wanted anything this badly. I lay in bed that night staring at the ceiling, trying my best to picture this God no one had ever really told me about. I came up with a thin and serious looking Santa Claus.

Yep, that is probably pretty much the way he looks, I thought, as I began to pray. "Dear God, please let me be the one picked for our basketball team. I'll be a good boy. I'll help Mom and Grandma around the house more. Really, I will, and well, it means a whole lot to me…Thanks."

Of course I did not tell God how impressed the girls at school would be if I made the team, especially Maureen. I had heard she kind of liked me, a little bit, anyway. Bolstered by my first conversation with God Almighty, I confidently dozed off, dreaming of shooting swishers that would triumphantly win games in the last three seconds. Glory would be mine as a superstar.

The next day I stood in front of the coach's office and read the ten names of the new team. The tenth name was David Betz, not Dick Bernal. My life crumbled before me. How could God do this to me? I decided God was either cruel or a poor judge of basketball talent. As everyone congratulated my pal David, I slunk down the hallway holding back tears of disappointment.

I decided later that day that if I was going to accomplish things in life, it would have to be on my own. I couldn't trust God or anyone else for help. I would make my own dreams come true!

> *There is a way that seems right to a man, but its*
> *end is the way of death.* ~PROVERBS 16:25

In 1957 we moved from sleepy little Watsonville to San Jose. I was coming of age as a teenager. The new fin-tailed car that Chevrolet put out was the talk of the town. That year Elvis belted out *"You Ain't Nothin' But a Hound Dog"* with his hips shimmying on the Ed Sullivan show.

As a lowly high school freshman, I wore my freshman's beanie cap to the football games and cheered louder than anyone else. I really wanted to feel accepted, but found myself the brunt of senior jokes and snickers instead.

The upperclassmen drove hot cars, shaved, and flexed their biceps at the girls. I'd pull up to school on my red bicycle, fighting pimples and sporting a chin covered with peach fuzz. My 126 pounds barely covered my six-foot frame.

In an effort to look cool, I'd don a rugged pair of blue jeans pegged just right, slip on a white T-shirt, and turn up the collar of my denim jacket. Add to that a little Clearasil, a waterfall hairdo, and a splash of cologne and maybe I could turn a girl's head, too.

It wasn't too long before I realized that my bike had to go. One day I gave it to a younger kid and started hoofing it to school.

About that time, my mother remarried. Her new husband was a nice man named Emmett, whose first wife was deceased. He had been left with four children, so all of us moved into the same house.

My oldest stepbrother, Fritz, had an old Ford pickup that begged me to hot-wire it. One night around midnight, my friend Les and I fired it up and took off for a spin. Les figured I knew how to drive, and I was sure he was a seasoned pro. We barreled along for two whole miles before the engine blew up. In a downpour of rain, we pushed the truck all the way back.

The sun peaked over the horizon as we inched the dead truck back up the sloping driveway, leaving it exactly where it had been parked before. Mom couldn't understand why Les and I slept in until noon. Poor old Fritz tinkered around out there for hours trying to figure out what had happened to his pride and joy.

I finally got up and made my way outside. Innocently, I strolled around the truck. Fritz stood there scratching his chin, but Emmett shot me a knowing glance that nearly stopped my heart. *My stepfather knew!*

Emmett really won me over when he winked to me, and then said to Fritz, "Well, son, I guess she just up and died."

LAZY J RANCH

The summer of 1960 was hot and long. I was too young to get a work permit. All my friends over sixteen were working at the local cannery making good money, enough to buy themselves cars. On Saturdays, they'd drive to school, wash and wax the love of their lives, and plan the strategy for cruising around town that night while I tagged along waving at the girls, and dreaming of the day when I could proudly weave through the drive-ins in my own car. Life was not fair.

Les dropped in one afternoon in July. "Ever hear of hops, Dickie?" he asked excitedly.

"Hops? What's hops?"

"My dad has arranged for you and me to work picking hops on his friend's ranch up near Sacramento for the rest of the summer!" he exclaimed. "They use hops for making beer. And if we work six days a week, ten hours a day, guess what?"

"We'll make enough money to buy a car?" I blurted out.

"Yup; more than $300 a month, I figured it out on paper."

Wow! We could both have cars by the time our junior year started. Now that made life worth living. Les and I were going to be sixteen and popular!

Mom and Grandma reluctantly agreed to let me go up to the hops ranch with Les. As we turned into the ranch's long, dusty driveway, the smell of freshly cut alfalfa hung thick in the afternoon air. "LAZY J RANCH" was painted on one of the large silos in the distance. The hops fields stretched out before us like an endless ocean of green.

When we walked into the employment trailer, a burly man named Sam stood up. He wore a faded flannel shirt rolled up past his bulging biceps. I could see an anchor tattooed on the back of his left hand. He had a couple of cigarettes tucked into his front shirt pocket. His weather-beaten cowboy hat looked cool.

"Hello boys," he said, extending a big hand. "You must be Les and Dick. Here are some papers to sign so we can get goin'."

Les' Dad had called ahead and made arrangements for us. We found out later that these arrangements included instructions to Sam to work us into the ground, and not let us get away with anything.

Sam drove us out to the fields and showed us where we would be loading hops onto the back of trucks. He said that the workday started with breakfast at 5:30 a.m. We'd be out in the fields by 6:30, get a thirty-minute break for lunch, and work until 5 p.m. Sam told us we had to wear gloves because of something called "hop poisoning," but I didn't dare ask him what that meant.

Bernal, how bad do you want a car? I asked myself. *The only way you're going to get one is to work your butt off.*

Sam drove us back over to the crew quarters. The interior looked like an army barracks with 20 cots lined up on each side. Sam picked us out two cots by the door. He pointed to the makeshift closet for our clothes. The toilets and showers looked pretty cramped.

"Supper's at 7:00 in the mess hall, boys," he said, leaving Les and me sitting on our bunks. The screen door creaked open and a group of men entered the barracks. Dusty and tired from their day in the hops fields, I noticed they were African-American or Mexican, no Caucasians in the bunch. They all were in their thirties or forties.

One by one they eyed us up and down. One said, "My, my, what have we here? What are your names, boys?"

I jumped up quickly and answered, "My name is Dickie, and this is my friend Les."

One six-foot-seven African-American said his name was Joe Brown. "Where you from?" Joe asked.

"San Jose," I said.

He laughed. "Well, I don't like the name 'Dickie', so I'm going to call you 'San Jose Slim.'" I found out later that Joe Brown wasn't just creative with nicknames. He could also quote Edgar Allan Poe and cite some Scripture.

I swallowed hard. "That's fine, sir. You can call me anything you want."

Just then the rest of the men came in. They looked real tough. I felt my stomach clench up. We found out later that all these guys were convicts out on work furlough to help support their families.

That night in the mess hall, Les whispered to me, "Can you believe this? Can you believe we're going to be living with these guys all summer long? Think we'll get hurt?"

A sense of optimism welled up inside me. I shrugged my shoulders. "Naw, we'll be all right. They seem to be a nice sort."

Les looked at me with disbelieving eyes. "Oh yeah?"

After dinner, we walked back to the barracks. Feeling a little timid, we walked up and down the aisle watching the men playing cards and shaking dice. One man strummed a guitar and another guy blew his harmonica. A few dozed in their bunks. Others simply stared up at the ceiling, deep in thought. We caught a few smiles as we walked around. I felt that they were taking to us. At least I hoped so.

The next day, the work supervisor put Les on one truck and me on another. When we came back in for lunch, I saw Les standing over by the office. I walked over and asked, "What are you doing?"

"I got fired this morning," he said. "I'm going back home. My folks are on the way to pick me up. Let's get out of this place!"

"Fired! How did you get fired?"

"Some guy said something to me that I didn't like." Les shook his head. "I talked back to him, and they fired me. So I'm going home. Are you ready to go?"

I thought about it, then said, "No, I'm not going anywhere. I came up here to work, and I want to make enough money for a car. Besides, I'm not a quitter."

Les shrugged. "Have it your way."

Later that afternoon, Les' parents arrived. In a flash he was gone. Now I was going this alone-with 29 African-American guys and one Mexican.

The men in the barracks chorused, "Hey, San Jose, what happened to your friend?"

"He got fired," I said. They all whooped with laughter.

"Well, boy," one man named Hammer chuckled, "you probably won't make it much longer yourself. This ain't work fit for a boy."

You just watch me, I thought. *I can hang in there with the toughest.*

That night, I went for a walk. Out under the stars I took a deep breath and gazed up at the heavens. "I will make it," I said out loud. "I will win."

On Sundays the men all went into town. That left me by myself in the barracks with nothing to do. I asked Sam if there was some way I could make a little extra money.

"Sure," he said. "You can scrub out the hoppers on Sunday. It's pretty hard work, but I'll pay you a little extra."

I took the job and started working ten hours on Sundays and a couple of hours overtime each night. It was grimy, back-breaking work, but the 1954 Oldsmobile of my dreams kept me going. That baby was going to cost me $400.00.

In the little spare time that I had, I learned how to box from a thin jive-talkin' guy named Calhoun. Calhoun was cool, streetwise, and about 24. He carefully combed his curly black hair, even though his clothes and shoes were tattered. When he'd talk about the past in New York City, his eyes would glaze over with the rough life he'd had. Calhoun always wanted to beat me at running or boxing, but he wasn't mean about it. I grew quite attached to Calhoun.

MY BROTHER'S KEEPER

At summer's end the hops season came to a close. The long hard days were finally over. I knew I was going to miss these guys. Joe Brown had become a kind of guardian angel. The guys who played guitar and harmonica had taught me several songs. Calhoun was like an older brother.

On the day I was to leave, my stepfather came to pick me up, and boy did his eyes get big when he saw my ethnic work mates. I hugged each one of them, saving Calhoun for last. There were some wet eyes. Mine among them.

18

An impulse came over me and I handed my duffel bag to Calhoun. In it were my leather work gloves, Red Wing work boots and work socks, my work shirt and jeans. I knew we were about the same size. Calhoun started crying and hugged me tightly. Brushing away a tear, I took off my white hard-hat, and placed it on his head. He smiled broadly.

I felt a tug on my heart that I'll never forget when I turned away and got in the car. I kept wondering what would become of my new-found friends. I felt a rush of frustration and empathy for all African-Americans and Mexicans, as if I was one of them suffering the pangs of bigotry and persecution. This experience awakened my first stirrings of compassion for people.

And I had learned something about myself – I could hang in there when things got tough. I would return to my junior year of high school as more of a veteran of life.

But this wasn't to last. The tender roots of self-dignity and caring for others were not deep enough to withstand the self-willed tempest of my roaring twenties.

Am I my brother's keeper? ~GENESIS 4:9

CHAPTER 2

ROARING TWENTIES

My high school graduation in 1962 coincided with a period of transition in America. If I had a time in my life that I could do over, it would be the years from 1962 to 1974. President John F. Kennedy was assassinated. America lost her innocence. And so did I. Then came Vietnam, the hippie movement, Watergate, the assassination of Martin Luther King, and the Charles Manson murders. Things got freaky.

The days of *Leave It to Beaver, Father Knows Best,* and *Mr. Ed* were long gone. The innocent themes of the music popular during my high school years were replaced by lyrics about rebellion and cynicism.

A friend got me a good job as an ironworker, making union wages. Monday through Friday I was a good ole' boy. But come Friday night, I would grab my bellbottoms, headband, and beads, and make the scene in San Francisco. My buddies and I hung out at Bill Graham's Fillmore West. Jimmy Hendrix. Janis Joplin. Grace Slick. Iron Butterfly. Country Joe and the Fish. Blue Cheer. We saw them all. I'd drop acid or swallow some magic mushrooms to soar with the music.

My favorite was *mescaline* in spite of the bitter pungent taste. This drug created a rushing sensation. Everywhere I looked colors became bright and vivid, probably because my pupils were so dilated. The mescaline made everything seem hysterically funny. The next morning my cheek muscles would be sore from laughing so hard. We'd take our reds to get off our whites and go listen to the blues. Some of these weekends turned into a blurred psychedelic haze.

Even though I was wreaking havoc on my body every weekend, I was taking karate to stay in shape. I studied at a Korean style dojo on Alameda Street in old San Jose. I earned a brown belt and became assistant instructor on Monday and Wednesday nights.

INSTRUCTOR TO THE HELL'S ANGELS

A bunch of Hell's Angels piled into the karate dojo one night. They told my instructor that they wanted to improve their street-fighting skills. The instructor assigned me the job of taking them through calisthenics and loosening them up with basic kicks.

After a few weeks, I started making friends with these guys. I was attracted by their loyalty and camaraderie, as misguided as it was. I was impressed that they would take a bullet for each other, and never rat on their buddies even if the police interrogated one. Oddly, the Hell's Angels provided my first example of a covenant in action - a kind of nothing-can-come-between-us fraternity.

I was lured closer to their lifestyle by the excitement that swirled around them. As a kid I had read Zane Grey and Louis L'Amour. These Hell's Angels seemed like a throwback to those Wild West days. They had their own rules and code of honor, spurning social norms. Yet there was an openness and transparency among them – a real bond of trust.

I drank and smoked dope at their parties, but got turned off when I'd see some of them jamming heroin needles into their arms. I remember one party in particular at a flophouse in Mountain View. The garage was filled with motorcycle parts. There wasn't any furniture to speak of because the house was used for parties.

About 100 people dropped by that night. Loud music rocked the house. A new keg of beer was rolled into the living room every few minutes. One guy rode his Harley-Davidson into the living room and did a *wheelie*, before roaring out the back door.

One of the leaders named Billy liked me, even though I was somewhat of an outsider. I found myself staring at his girl-friend, who was a real knockout. A guy could get killed for doing something that stupid. Billy noticed me leering at her. But instead of getting mad, he walked over and offered her to me.

At that very moment I had taken a drag off an opium pipe. Within seconds I felt frozen against the wall. It took my total concentration to keep from falling on my face. Billy's girlfriend came over to ask if I was ready for her. I just gave her a glassy-eyed stare. I stood glued to the wall from one until five in the morning. I never tried opium again.

It wasn't long before I came to a crossroads with these guys. My Hell's Angels group came in for a karate lesson livid with rage. One of their bikes had been stolen. They had reconnoi-tered the area and found the bike. Leaving it there, they planned to go back and set a trap for the thieves.

"Hey Dick, you wanna have some fun tonight?"

"Sure," I said.

So there I was in a '52 Chevy torpedo-back, 50 yards from where the bike was hidden. We were crouched down low in the car. *This is really cool,* I thought. Just then I heard clicking sounds in the front and back seats. They were shoving magazines into pistols and talking about how they were going to kill the enemy.

My Grandma's voice went off in my head and I pictured her no-nonsense gaze: *"Dicky, you shouldn't be here. Now you get out of this mess before you end up in jail!"*

I said to the Man upstairs, if He existed, "Oh, get me outta this!" But I was too afraid to leave. I gabbed my way through the night, pretending everything was fine. Miraculously, nobody showed up. When the sun came up and I was able to leave the car, I vowed to ease out of my gang involvement over the next month. Since that time about five of the guys I knew have died, including Billy.

〜

After a couple of years, all the deafening rock concerts started sounding alike to me. One night, a friend and I were listening to a band in San Francisco, when a young man followed me into the restroom. He wanted to sell me some hits of methadone. He was about nineteen, pleasant looking, but his brain was fried. I could barely make out his words as he stuttered and struggled to communicate. He had "tombstones in his eyes," as one rock song of the day said.

Bernal, I said to myself, *it's time to find a new way of living before you end up like this poor soul.*

During this time, the *Jesus Movement* had broken out. Hundreds of zealots flooded the streets passing out tracts and witnessing. A group of former addicts approached me one night in front of the fairgrounds. They could see I was hell-bound, but boy, did they scare me! They were wild-eyed, shouting the name of Jesus, and wanting to cast devils out of me. "Join us, brother. Leave the world of sin behind. Come be like us; free! Jesus loves you, brother!"

"Uh, hey, I'm happy for you guys, really. It's great that you fellows have found religion. But I have to go. I have a really important appointment."

I needed to do some more research in living by my own rules and passions.

> *Since they didn't bother to acknowledge God,*
> *God quit bothering them and let them run loose.*
> *And then all hell broke loose.* ~ROMANS 1:28-29
> THE MESSAGE

RHYTHM & BOOZE

One evening I visited Dad at his house. He downed a few double shots of whiskey, then started lecturing me about how to fight. "Never kick a man in a fight," he declared.

"Why?" I asked. "A fight is a fight."

"If you're going to hit someone, hit him with your fist like a man. If I ever hear of you using your feet, I'll come after you and whip you myself."

Surprising myself, I fired back, "Oh, yeah? And who is going to help you?"

I had never talked back to Dad before. He looked stunned. We stared at each other like the gunfighters in *High Noon*. Casually, he tossed down another two fingers of whiskey and stood up. I tossed back my shot and stood up.

Dad's girlfriend came running out of the kitchen and tried to calm us down, but it was too late.

"So you think you're pretty quick, huh?" he challenged. "Then show me your stuff, boy." He got into a Jack Dempsey stance.

Great, this is just great, I said to myself. *What now, big mouth. If I sit down, he'll think I'm a sissy. If I accept his challenge, someone might get hurt. Boy! I forgot how big Dad is.*

"Dad, let me demonstrate what I've learned in karate. I am going to kick you lightly under your left armpit. It'll be so fast you can't block it, so just relax and don't move. Okay?"

My somewhat amused father replied, "Really? When are you going to do all this?"

"Now," I yelled. I spun around with a wheel-kick. But I'd had just enough liquor to throw off my timing. The powerful kick struck my dad squarely in the side, breaking three of his ribs. He wheezed and dropped like a sack of potatoes.

Dad lay there grasping his side for a moment, and then broke into a pained laugh. "Boy, you're quick as lightning," he croaked. "You think you could teach me that kick some day?"

A flood of mixed emotions hit me! I felt like dirt for decking my Dad, yet I was proud for gaining his respect.

"RIDE 'EM COWBOY"

Later, I tried a different tack for getting closer to my father. Dad had been involved with horses and rodeos all his life. Yep, I got a pair of cowboy boots, some Wranglers, a sharp-looking Stetson, a buck stitch belt, and tried myself out on the rodeo circuit.

I signed up at a local rodeo and rode a big Brahma bull. To my utter astonishment, I hung on to the ornery thing for the full 8 seconds! I liked the applause, too. So I figured I would get real good at rodeoing, then invite the old man out to see me perform. Dad had always wanted me to be a cowboy like him, and I needed his acceptance really bad. I felt obsessed with the notion of becoming my dad's friend.

After a few months of jackpot bull riding, I had visions of going professional and making a living out of it. Now seemed the time to drop in on Dad. One Saturday, I stopped by his place to see how he was doing.

When he opened the front door his jaw dropped. He looked me over from top to bottom. "What ya been up to, cowboy?" he asked, grinning like a possum. He seemed pleased with my new choice of attire.

"Oh, just a little rodeoing," I said. "I like bull riding best."

"Really?" Dad sounded surprised. "I'd like to come take a look sometime."

My heart quickened. I finally had his attention. "Well, come Friday I'll be riding out at the Rocking R Ranch," I said, trying to cover my excitement.

"I know the place," he said. "I'll be there."

I could hardly believe it. In all the years that I had played sports in grammar and high school, Dad never once came to watch or cheer me on. When teammates would ask where he was, I'd say he was too busy working, knowing all the while that he was drunk or out womanizing.

Friday night came and I bolstered my confidence with a half-pint of blended whiskey. I scanned the stands for my dad. There he was, all decked out in western finery, sitting with his girlfriend Julie.

My first draw was a young bull called BOOGER RED. He had a bad reputation for scraping off riders along the fence. I eased down on the bull and wrapped the bucking rope around my left hand, thinking, how am I going to keep RED from heading for the fence?

"Ready, Dick?" shouted the handler.

"Outside!" I yelled, having taken that phrase from a real cowboy.

I do not know to this day what got into that crazy bull, but he jumped like a frog and landed on all fours, jarring every bone in my body. Then he did a 180-degree turn and jumped right back into the chute. I sailed right off him when he stopped, landing head first in six inches of wet manure.

Above the laughter of the crowd, I could hear my dad howling with glee, slapping his leg as if he had just seen the funniest thing in his life. "Ride'm, cowboy," he yelled. I sat up and did the only thing I could. I laughed too.

I decided the cowboy life was not for me. But more than that, I learned that I was barking up the wrong tree in striving to get my earthly father's approval.

In my late twenties I moved in with another bachelor named Jerry. He had just gone through a divorce and welcomed my company. I was trying to offset my lonely feelings. Before long Jerry's place was buzzing with booze, pot, and loud music. If life was a cruel joke, at least we could make up our own punch lines.

Foot loose and fancy free, I had quit pursuing and even speaking to my dad. The swinging bachelor's life was for me. No nagging wife making me come home right after work. No kids dragging me down to the ballpark, —just me to make happy.

I liked coming and going as I pleased and spending all my money on myself. I went out with a different girl whenever I wanted. I was the envy of all the guys at work. If there was a heaven on earth, this was surely it.

Yeah? Then why did I feel so miserable? Deep down inside, I had to admit that I really did want someone to come home to every night. I wanted to care and be cared for. I needed love.

My attempt at marriage at nineteen had been an absolute flop. The word *commitment* was not in my vocabulary. To me, the bond between a man and a woman was a physical thing that lasted for a short while until things got boring. I had no idea about the work and effort that makes for a successful marriage. Out of the failure of my first marriage, for which I take full blame, came a beautiful child who today has grown into a fine young man.

When Adam was a young boy, I felt uneasy around him. I felt guilty for doing the same thing to him that my dad had done to me. But I had no power to break the curse over my life. The sins of my father had been passed down once again. I figured I had made my own bed, so I had to accept my fate.

Bernal, I thought, *you're incapable of having a normal family life, just like your dad. You will undoubtedly die young, so live hard and fast, and get it all before it gets you.*

I hadn't spoken to Dad in eight months. When I'd gone back to wearing my hippie outfit with long hair and bellbottoms, he had blown his stack. "Don't ever come to visit me looking like that!" he yelled. So I didn't. Our yelling match left us both too proud to make amends.

I was shocked beyond belief when Dad died of a heart attack in December of 1970. He was only in his mid-fifties, but the wear and tear of his rough lifestyle got the best of him. One minute he was in the world, a phone call away, and the next minute he was gone forever.

The finality of his death really hit me when I saw Dad laying in the coffin at his funeral three days later. I felt cheated that he'd died before I had the chance to remedy our rift. *Where is Dad now?* I wondered. I surely hoped he was in heaven and not in hell.

At the funeral, my step-brother Chris looked dreadful. He couldn't believe our dad had died. That week he became deeply depressed, even suicidal. I think the first pastoring I ever did was putting my arm around Chris' shoulder and comforting him. But I didn't have any real tools for helping people. So I bought him a six-pack to ease his despair. Still, I cared more about helping him through his dark valley than attending to my own pain.

Our family doctor had pointed out that heart disease ran in the male members of my family. Most had died young. My dad's first heart attack had been 12 years earlier.

The doctor had picked up the pattern of high blood pressure and a fluttering heart when I was 19. My smoking and drug and alcohol use didn't help my occasional dizziness and heart palpitations.

The memory of Dad continued to linger. And, on the heels of his death, a couple of years later, Grandma Lu died. She meant so much to me. We had a high regard for Mom because she worked to support the family, but the everyday nurturing, discipline and good Christian values came from Grandma.

Grandpa had died four months earlier and we all saw what his death had done to Grandma. She was so lonely that we believe she died of a broken heart.

Boy, life without these significant family members around was beginning to affect me. When death hits so close to home, one's perspective in life has a way changing – I was now searching for meaning to life.

My Twilight Encounter

One night in early 1974 1 was awakened out of a very deep sleep. Adrenalin rushed through me, and a sense of alarm gripped me as I lay there with eyes open, feeling a strange sensation passing through my toes and feet. This electric tingling began to creep up my legs until it reached my lower back, and then it stopped momentarily. My whole lower body felt numb and lifeless. Slowly the sensation began to crawl almost animal-like up my spine. *What in the world was happening to me? Dear God, I'm not dreaming. This is real!*

Eventually, the sensation reached the base of my neck. An explosion of crimson flashed across my vision. There was no pain. Then brilliant red turned to black. The next thing I knew I was hovering like a hummingbird over my body, looking down at what had been Dick Bernal.

How sad he looks, I thought.

I was hovering about 18 inches below the ceiling of my bedroom, totally aware of my surroundings, and looking down on the body that housed Dick Bernal. I thought to myself, *Bernal, your body is dead, but you are still alive. Now what?* I wondered. *Where am I going? Will someone come for me?*

I felt free, yet perplexed. As I pondered my predicament I began to sink, pulled back down into my body by a strange force. I reentered my body right through the chest area. The next thing I knew, I was lying flat on my back in bed staring up at the ceiling.

Life began to flow back into my body. In an exact reversal of the previous process, the tingling sensation at the base of my neck progressed down my spine and into my legs.

I jumped out of bed, turned on all the lights, and flipped on the television. I sat down and nervously lit a cigarette. For three hours I sat deep in thought, smoking and shaking my head in disbelief. Finally, the rays of the early morning sun broke over the Mount Hamilton range. I got dressed and ready for work.

I drove to Stanford University where I was overseeing a hospital remodeling project. I was convinced that I had had a stroke and died, but for some unexplainable reason I was still alive.

Years later, I told Carla about the whole experience. "Honey," she said, "the Lord spared your life. He knew that you would accept His call to the ministry."

My heart is severely pained within me, and the terrors of death have fallen upon me. ~PSALMS 55:4

CHAPTER 3

APPOINTMENT WITH THE FUTURE

Life seemed bleak at 30. I was still living like a nomad, everything I owned fit into the trunk of my car. I felt out of touch with my twelve-year-old son, who was being reared by another man. My friends were all alcoholics or addicts. On top of that, my job as an ironworker was for very young men. I had maybe another 10 years before my back would give out.

I felt that if I went to one more party, I was headed for a jump off the Golden Gate Bridge. My favorite whiskey now tasted like battery acid. The girls in the clubs all looked and sounded alike. Like soulless mannequins, they'd whisper to every lonely Joe, *"Hey, what's your name? I'll bet you are a Leo. Wanna have some fun?"* Egads! Wasn't there anything more to life?

The day after a lackluster Christmas in 1974, my roommate and I were at our local watering hole drinking long-neck *Budweisers*, playing pool, and listening to Merle, Waylon, and Willie sing about their problems.

"I'm sick of this place, Jerry," I said, feeling the post-holiday blues. "Let's go somewhere else. I need a change of scenery tonight."

There was a nicer place right up the road where a different crowd hung out. We pulled into the parking lot, and I wondered why there were only one or two cars.

"Is it closed?" I asked.

"Well, we'll soon find out," said Jerry. He jumped out and tried the front door.

"They're open," he shouted as he motioned me to follow him. When we walked in, the bartender looked pleased that someone had showed up.

"What brings you boys out tonight?" he asked cheerfully.

"Just looking for a little after-Christmas action," said Jerry.

"Boy, you two sure picked the wrong night. Everyone is at home resting up for New Year's Eve."

Just then the door opened. In walked two very attractive girls. Jerry and I grinned at the bartender, who winked back. Jerry elbowed me to go into action with my smooth operator routine, which I'd done dozens of times before. No big deal. I'd walk up to a ladies' table, introduce myself, and ask one of them to dance.

I headed straight for the red-head facing me. "Hi. Would you like to dance with me?"

"No, thanks," she said. "I'm married."

"Oh, too bad. How about you?" I asked the other one whose back had been turned to me.

"No, thanks," she said, still with her back to me, and staring at the other girl.

I liked her long blonde hair and persisted. "Come on, let's dance." My insides yelled at me that she wasn't interested and to beat it. But somehow I wouldn't budge. I had seen other guys pester pretty girls and had gotten in more than one fight coming to their rescue. Here I was doing exactly what I hated, but for some strange reason, I could not leave that table. What was wrong with me?

"Please, just one dance-pretty please?"

As I bent over the table, the gold cross I wore around my neck fell out of my unbuttoned shirt. I felt that if a cross was good enough for Elvis and Tom Jones to wear, why not me?

The blonde woman stared at the cross and said, "Okay. Just one."

As she stood up, I noticed how pretty she was, a real angel to me. The band was playing short versions of old standards, probably because of the empty dance floor. The music stopped much too quickly. Just my luck!

"What's your name?" I asked hurriedly as she sat down.

"Carla, and this is my sister, Karen. We haven't seen each other for a long time, so we're catching up on family news. Thank you, Good-bye."

"Hey, why don't I join you, and you can talk all you want?"

The whole time I was saying to myself, *Bernal, don't be a jerk. Leave these two sweet sisters alone. You're bugging them. It's obvious they have other things on their minds.*

But no, I pulled up a chair and sat down next to them. I smiled as they went on and on about family events. When I'd put in my two-cents they'd offer polite smiles and continue talking to each other. As the evening wore on, it was getting time for working people to go home. I asked Carla if she wanted to have dinner with me the next night. She stared at me without saying anything. But when I suggested Chinese food, she said that Chinese was her favorite.

"Great," I said. "Give me your address and phone number. I'll call right before I drop by."

Carla told me later that she said to Karen on their way home, "Why did I say yes? I'm not looking for anyone, nor do

I want to go out with him tomorrow night."

The next night I found myself sharing with this beautiful stranger my dream of a normal life —marriage, children, a house with a picket fence, a vegetable garden, dogs and cats, the whole bit. I shared my past failures and my fears of an uncertain future. I unashamedly bared my heart and soul to her.

For some reason, it was so easy to talk to her. There was something different about this woman that I couldn't put my finger on. I had prided myself on my knowledge of women. Being around more women than men most of my life, I felt I pretty much understood their ways, moods, and mannerisms. But I had never encountered this kind of girl before. It was not just her looks, because I had dated very good-looking girls. It was deeper than that. She had this warm inner glow. Her sister had it too. I wondered what it was.

The following Saturday, I had extra tickets to a concert in Berkeley, so I asked Carla if she and her sister wanted to go. The two girls piled into my coupe and we headed for the concert. Actually, I had a date with another girl who was waiting for me in front of the theater. As awkward as all this was, I had not wanted to miss a chance to be with Carla. Everyone made the best of the situation and we all walked in together.

As the days and weeks passed, Carla and I became virtually inseparable. One day, some of her relatives arrived from Oklahoma. Carla invited me to a barbecue at her mother's house in Hayward. She had neglected to tell me, however, that these were all church-going people. In I waltzed with my customary case of beer, a gallon of cheap wine, and a trusty cigarette dangling out of the corner of my mouth. In my circle of friends, you never showed up for a party empty-handed.

35

I never saw so much iced tea and soft drinks in all my life! I was the only one smoking and drinking. Still, I had a great time talking sports, construction work, and fishing with the visiting male relatives. They seemed to enjoy my company, and I felt completely at home. Carla seemed proud showing off her new beau.

As Carla and I were getting ready to leave, her mother followed us out to the car and said, "Daddy and I are surely praying for you kids."

Driving Carla home to her sister's, I could not shake those words out of my mind—"We are praying for you." No one had ever told me, "I am praying for you." Someone was talking to God about *me*. How about that!

The next Saturday Carla was cutting my hair. "Honey," I said, "tell me about the Bible and church. What is a Baptist anyway?"

She began to share a little about Jesus. Then she dropped a Bible in my lap. I handled it cautiously at first, then began to leaf through it as if I knew exactly what I was doing.

I thought to myself, *How do you pronounce "Deuteronomy"? For goodness sakes, how can anyone understand this stuff.* I flipped to another book of the Old Testament, *"Numbers." Hmmm, —man, how does this relate to anything? This is 1975. I guess some people get something out of this, but I'm not one of them.*

"What do you think?" Carla asked excitedly.

"I will have to really get into this later," I lied. *Much later,* I thought to myself.

Our love grew deeper over that year. My son Adam approved wholeheartedly of Carla, and she fell in love with him. On November 29, 1975, we exchanged our vows in front of the Rev. Johnny B. Love, who married us in Lake Tahoe, Nevada.

A couple of friends joined us for the celebration. As the minister was reading the vows, I could tell Carla was listening intently to the Bible passages. I just wanted to finish the *"I do"* part and get on with the party.

My little wife looked so beautiful and radiant. I was fighting the flu, but still had a great time.

Gone were my carefree bachelor days, and I had no regrets. Carla was a stabilizing factor in my life. The following morning a foot of new snow had fallen in the Tahoe Basin. The sun broke through by 9a.m. What a splendid sight. Who knows? Maybe this beautiful day was a sign of things to come —a fresh, clean start.

> *He who finds a wife finds a good thing, and obtains favor from the LORD.* ~PROVERBS 18:22

GIVEN A SECOND CHANCE

Soon after our marriage, my construction company sent me further north in California to oversee some projects. Carla and I picked a small mountain hamlet called Paradise for our new home. We had saved enough money to make a down payment on a cute little house tucked back in the forest.

I cut down on my drinking and came home from work like other married men. There was hunting and fishing right outside my back door. Fresh mountain air and folksy neighbors added to our contentment. Even the gas station attendant took time for a chat, and the waitresses at the local coffee shop called us by name.

On Saturdays Carla and I — accompanied by Trouble, our Brittany spaniel — would launch our aluminum boat into Lake Oroville and catch bass all day long. This was life! A good woman, a change of scenery, a faithful bird dog, and a place to call my own was all I needed for happiness.

Apparently, though, Carla didn't feel as euphoric. She began acting strange. I'd catch her staring into space and being somewhat distant. "What's wrong, honey?" I'd ask.

"Oh, nothing," she'd say. "Just thinking, that's all. No big deal."

Now and then she would disappear into the bedroom while I was watching the evening news, and I'd catch her reading her Bible. Occasionally I'd waken at 3:00 in the morning and find her on her knees by the side of the bed, crying and talking softly to God.

What is wrong with this woman? I fretted. *I'm giving her everything she could possibly want. Now what? And why does she need to pray like that? Nighttime is for sleeping.*

I didn't have the heart to tell her that praying was a waste of time. After all, God didn't help me make the basketball team back in the sixth grade, so why would He help her? Driving to work some mornings, I would think, *What a strange bunch of kinfolks I've got. But they sure seem happy, so maybe they do have something I don't have. I'll just let it slide.*

One night I came home and Carla greeted me at the door, her eyes dancing. "Guess what?" she asked excitedly.

"What?"

"Guess!" she repeated.

"Carla, I'm not in the mood for *Twenty Questions*. I'm tired, dear. I've had a hard day."

"Sit down," she said. "I have news for you."

"Now what? Are we being audited by the I.R.S.?"

"We're going to have a baby!"

A tidal wave of emotions cascaded through me; joy, an awareness of responsibility, a fear of change, then more joy.

"Really?" I blurted out. "When?" "Around Christmas," beamed my wife.

That night I sat up late thinking, *Dick, you've been given a second chance. Now don't blow this one. You are going to be a father again, and this time you're not a crazy nineteen-year-old. You are almost 32. It's time to grow up and be everything to this child that you are supposed to be—everything that your dad never was to you.*

THE MALLARDS WERE SURRENDERING

To me, fall was the best season in Paradise. The trees exploded with brilliant hues of red, orange, and sunburst yellow. The air was crisp. The sky turned cobalt blue with billowing clouds floating overhead like massive ships. There was a great duck club down in Woodland, about 80 miles south. The reports from the State Department of Fish and Game looked good. I felt excited. Plenty of ducks and geese were flocking to the lakes and fields.

The season began, but I stayed home on weekends with Carla, my sense of loyalty telling me to take care of her. At night I'd sit in front of the roaring fireplace, clean my shotgun and count the shells I had left from the year before. Between sips of coffee I scratched ole' Trouble's floppy ears. My dog seemed to sense that his favorite time of year was upon us. He'd sniff my 12-gauge shotgun and wag his tail with anticipation.

Carla, now seven-and-a-half months along, would sit in her favorite chair with her lap full of baby books. "Come feel the baby kicking!" she'd squeal every now and then. I would jump up and lay my hand on her belly. Even after dozens of times, a thrill kept zipping through me.

One weekend toward the end of the season, one of my buddies named Curt called. "Bernal, you should have seen the mallards today," he said. "We didn't even have to use our guns - they just surrendered and landed in the back of the pickups."

"Good-bye, Curt. Thanks for calling, pal," I grumbled, as I hung-up on my laughing friend.

"Why don't you go hunting with the guys?" asked Carla. "I'm not going to have the baby yet. If anything happens, I know how to reach you."

"You hear that, Trouble?" I asked my dog. He wagged his tail. "We're going hunting, boy!"

THE STORK ARRIVED EARLY

That Friday night I drove south and joined the guys at our duck club meeting. We played cards, drank a couple of bottles of brandy, and tapped our toes to Country music until 1:00 a.m.

The alarm went off at 4:00 a.m. on Saturday morning. I clambered into my gear, feeling the dull pound in my temples of a hangover. We drove out to the blind, camouflaged the dogs, poured ourselves cups of steaming hot coffee, and got our duck calls ready. Just as the sun began to make its morning climb, a flock of ducks appeared high above our pond, looking for a place to land.

My heart pounded with adrenaline. Then I looked across the way. *Who is that nut out there with his pickup lights on? This is private property. No vehicles are allowed. He's scaring all the ducks away. Of all the nerve! Who is that guy?*

Dick, a familiar voice called out, a shadowy figure approached through the mist. It was Carl, the dog trainer who got me into the club a few years back. "Her water broke, Dick," he called.

"What?"

"You're about to become a father," Carl announced, as deadpan as ever.

"My gosh!" I hollered as I ran to my truck. "Where is my truck?" *Oh, great. J.W.'s wife borrowed it.* "J.W.," I shouted, "give me your keys, man, quick. Come on, I'm about to be a father!"

Hysterical laughter erupted from each blind. I jumped into J.W.'s old Chevy pickup that would not go more than 60 miles-an-hour. It took 90 minutes to get to Feather River Hospital.

Completely forgetting that I had on a full set of waders, I waddled straight into the maternity ward—duck calls, hat, shotgun, shells, gloves, and all. When the nurse saw me, she broke into laughter. "He's here!" she yelled to the other nurses.

I didn't find much humor in any of this. As they led me into Carla's room, I felt relieved to see that she had not delivered yet. She was just starting labor.

"Sorry, sweetheart," she grinned. "Didn't mean to mess up your hunting trip."

"Hey, don't worry about it. I'm glad I'm here."

I was starting to feel a little silly about my get-up. The nurse said, "Mr. Bernal, why don't you go on home? It will be hours yet, and her sister is here to keep her company. Go get some rest, you look as if you could use it."

Back home I was too keyed-up to sleep. I kept my eye on the phone while doing a few chores. Finally, around 4:30 p.m. the nurse declared, "It's time, Mr. Bernal."

Carla and I had attended classes on natural childbirth, so I knew what to do when I got there. But while I was coaching Carla, my body realized just how tired it was. I couldn't stop yawning. The doctor saw my fatigue and recommended that I use his office couch to catch a wink or two of sleep. He assured me it would be an hour or so before the delivery.

Carla, who had been counting on me to coach her through the delivery, had to rely on her sister Karen, while her Prince Charming *sawed logs,* sound asleep, in the office next door.

Finally, the doctor came and shook my shoulder. "It's time, Dick," he announced. I followed him into the room where my wife was huffing and puffing through the final pangs of labor. I tried to help, but there was no time left. In the next instant my baby girl slipped into the world! Carla and I cried openly. "Sarah. We'll call her Sarah," we agreed.

That night I sat up late with ole' Trouble. It felt good to be alive.

I wonder if all that praying Carla did paid off? I asked myself.

I was beginning to believe in miracles. I had just witnessed one—a human birth coupled with a supernatural presence. It took more than human effort to create that beautiful baby!

Though weak from the birth, Carla whispered, "Thank you,

Jesus," over and over again.

> *To everything there is a season...a time to be*
> *born.* ~ECCLESIASTES 3:2

A few days after Sarah's birth, I had to work on a job in Sacramento. The carpenter foreman shouted at me from below the wall I was reinforcing. "Hey, Bernal, there's an emergency call for you down in the office."

Oh, no, I thought. *Not the baby, not Sarah.* I grabbed the phone.

Karen told me that Carla had been taken back to the hospital for profuse hemorrhaging.

"I'll be right there," I said. I flew out of the office. Paradise seemed like a million miles away. My wife needed me as never before. In my frustration, I cursed and beat my fist against the dashboard. I was driving at top speed, yet felt like I was crawling the 100-mile distance.

A stream of thoughts rushed through my mind. *What am I going to do when I get there? What can I say? What if she is dead?* I suddenly felt angry at that God of hers. Here I was a drinking, smoking, cursing heathen—and I was healthy as a horse. But my poor little wife, who was a God-fearing, Bible-reading woman, was bleeding to death.

"It's not fair," I ranted. "It is just not fair!"

I ran every red traffic light and ignored every speed limit sign. When the hospital finally came into sight, I began to tremble with desperation.

Why do people have to die?

Who designed this thing called life?

Why are there so many complications attached to it?
If God's in charge, then why do people suffer?
Dare I pray for Carla?
Would God even listen to someone like me?

At my wits end, I quit thinking and started praying. "God, Jesus, Whoever You are, please help Carla. I beg You, please heal my wife. She truly loves You and talks about You to me. I know I don't deserve an audience with You, but if You can find it in Your heart to do this, I will do whatever You want. I will. I promise. Thank You for hearing me out."

I pulled into the hospital parking lot where a few days before we'd felt unspeakable joy in carrying our baby daughter out to the car. I double-parked and ran to the emergency entrance. I kept telling myself that everything was going to be all right.

Our doctor met me outside Carla's room. I could tell by his expression that things were not going well.

"Dick, we've got a major problem."

He went on to explain that a piece of the placenta had not been expelled after Sarah's birth. Ten days later, when it had broken loose, it had torn a main artery. They couldn't seem to stop the hemorrhaging. They had already done a dilation and curettage procedure. Now they were thinking of a complete hysterectomy.

Carla looked horrible when I walked into her room. Yellow skin, chalk white lips; she looked like a corpse. Nurses were working frantically to get her blood pressure up, but it was steadily dropping.

"I'm sorry, honey," she whispered as if she had done something wrong.

Wanting to give reassurance, I patted her gently on the head. "Don't worry you're going to be fine. What are you sorry for, anyway? It's not your fault."

On the doctor's orders, I left the hospital room and drove to Karen's house. She was looking after Sarah. I felt an incredible fatherly urge to hold my daughter. I cuddled little Sarah in a rocking chair and chucked her under the chin. "Your mom is in a bit of a jam right now," I whispered. "What do you think about all this? Do you think it's going to be okay? Yeah, I think so, too. I wish I was as peaceful as you are right now."

Every time the phone rang, I flinched, wanting to answer it, yet afraid of what I might hear. News had spread to family and friends in the Bay Area, so the calls were coming in fast and furious. Even my crusty iron-working buddies were calling with concern in their voices. They offered help, money, and even their own blood if necessary. The next voice I heard was the doctor's, saying that they were going to decide on the hysterectomy in the morning.

I hardly slept at all. The next morning, Karen and I anxiously waited outside Carla's room for the news. Silently and hardly breathing, I repeated my promise to God.

The doctor walked out of Carla's room and turned to us. He was beaming. "We seem to have had some kind of a miracle here," he said. "Last night, the blood flow suddenly stopped. I can't explain it, but I can tell you that we have a rapidly recovering young woman on our hands, and she's very hungry." I raced into the room. There was my wife smiling and sitting up.

*Let us therefore come boldly to the throne of
grace that we may obtain mercy and find grace to*

help in time of need. ~HEBREWS 4:16

MY VOW TO GOD

On Christmas Eve morning I drove down to the Feather River Hospital to pick up Carla. Walking across the parking lot toward the hospital entrance, I stopped, gazed up at the stars, and said out loud, "Thank you, God."

I felt good saying thank you, but then I remembered my impulsive promise to God. "If You will heal Carla, I will do anything You ask of me," I had vowed.

What on earth can God do with me? I puzzled. *Nothing; I'm not in His league.* I shrugged my shoulders and walked on. I purposely didn't tell Carla about my deal with God. I knew she took God seriously, and I didn't want her to use my promise as leverage to get me into a church.

For the next several weeks, I tried to get back into my usual routine - work, family, and a few beers to ease the tensions. But I kept thinking about God. *Who is God, anyway? Why is there a God? Where did He come from?* I would catch myself staring at the sky and wondering about the place called heaven.

One clear Saturday in January, toward the end of duck season, I sat in my blind watching the geese and ducks migrate south. *Why do they do that? Is there really a God who controls nature? Even this ant crawling across my boot seems to have a purpose in life. Amazing! I wonder where I fit in.*

That Friday I came home to the aroma of my favorite stew. "Hope you're hungry, honey," said Carla. "I made this specially for you."

"Great," I said. "I'm famished. Listen, dear, I am going to

the club in the morning. It's the last week of duck season. But I'll come home tomorrow night, and we can go to church Sunday morning. What do you think?"

"Really? Honest? Oh, honey, this is great. God has answered my prayers."

I hope she understands I'm not going to make a habit of it, I thought. *I just want to make good on my promise to God by showing up once to His house.*

On Sunday morning I stood in front of my closet looking over my limited wardrobe. *What do people wear to church?* I wondered. My collection of work and hunting/fishing attire did not include any Sunday suits. My eyes fell on my Tom Jones style lightning-blue jumpsuit. *That'll look nice.* I put it on even though it fit a little tight. *What else?* I thought. *Oh yes—how about this electric green Elvis Presley shirt. Perfect. I'll unbutton the top to show off my gold chain and cross.* I completed the ensemble with a pair of TONY LAMA ostrich skin boots.

Carla was so excited that she could care less how I looked. Little Sarah was very pretty in a new pink dress.

Carla had spotted a nice little denominational church, so that is where we went. As we walked in, I noticed a lot of older folks. I had always loved senior citizens, probably because of my great respect for my grandparents. The gentleman next to me was really old, maybe 90. His eyes were closed and his head lay back in an unorthodox position for church. In fact, he looked dead. I watched him for a long time wondering, *Is this guy breathing?*

After a few songs out of a book they called a hymnal, the preacher started in. He was a nice, safe-looking man who seemed at peace with himself. He spoke of God's goodness and mercy as if he really knew all about it first hand. About halfway through the message, the old man next to me snorted out loud and took a deep breath. I almost jumped out of my skin, but I was very relieved to know he was alive.

Carla thought I wasn't too impressed with the service. After we were dismissed, she began inquiring about any nearby churches with people closer to our ages. A sweet little old lady suggested a church of another denomination that was right up the road. She said that we would find a much younger congregation.

"Well?" Carla asked, as we started for home. "What did you think?"

"I liked it," I said. "It felt good."

Somewhat surprised but encouraged, she pressed her advantage and said, "How about next Sunday? Do you want to try the other church?"

"Sure," I replied. "Why not?" Actually, I had gotten excited about this new adventure of hunting for God, but I wasn't going to let her see my enthusiasm.

The next Sunday we drove into the packed parking lot of a large, impressive looking church. Carla carried Sarah in, saying, "Here, hold my Bible while I find the nursery."

Man, it felt strange to carry a Bible. I felt a little embarrassed, like I do when I'm holding my wife's purse and she's trying on dresses. *Won't everybody stare at me?* Then I saw several men carrying Bibles. That helped me out a little.

A big, rough-looking guy stood in the church doorway shaking hands with everyone who passed. *How about that?* I thought. *Churches even have doormen.*

"Now, who do we have here?" he asked as we entered the

lobby

My wife answered. "I'm Carla, this is little Sarah, and this is my husband, Dick."

Before I knew it, his big hand had grabbed mine. "What do you do for a living, Dick?"

"I'm a rod buster," I responded. "We're remodeling the State Capitol Building."

"An ironworker!" he barked. "I don't like ironworkers. I'm a carpenter."

I just stared at him until he broke into a belly laugh. His laughter subsided into a warm smile and he patted me on the back. I felt genuinely welcomed to church by this man's man.

"I like that guy," I whispered to Carla. We found seats and listened to the choir and some announcements. For the next forty minutes, I sat mesmerized by the words coming from a handsome, silver-haired pastor. He talked about how people could make a U-turn from self-centered living to a life of trusting God and serving others. He said that God sent His Son Jesus into the world to make friends with us and save us from sin and hell. I began to perspire. I couldn't escape the fact that the pastor was inviting me to come face to face with God and own up to the way I'd been living.

The pastor closed by asking everyone to bow their heads and close their eyes. I wanted to make a beeline for the men's room, anything to get out of there. Next the pastor asked if there was anyone who would like to come down to the altar to accept Jesus into their hearts. My body froze, as if paralyzed, because I realized that the choice was mine.

Carla was affected differently. She jumped to her feet. "Come on, honey, let's go," she exclaimed as she grabbed my arm. She tried to pull me out into the aisle. "Let's go, Dick!"

"What are you doing, woman?" I said a bit too loud. "Let go of my arm!"

I felt my face heating up. The people around us were smiling and nodding as if to say, "Do it. Go to the altar with your wife."

My bull-headedness miffed Carla. "Well, I'm going by myself," she said, and off she headed up the aisle toward the preacher.

I felt totally exposed before the whole world. I watched a lady counselor take Carla to a back room. All kinds of thoughts began rushing through my mind. *What were they doing to her back there? What is she saying to them?* I had read about weird cults that entrapped people. I thought about finding Sarah and running out of the building.

Just then, Carla appeared from a side door, beaming from ear to ear. She walked back to our aisle and hugged me. "I did it, honey," she said. "I rededicated my life to Jesus. I feel great. I wish you had come with me."

"I suppose you gave our house away and all our savings," I said, trying to put a damper on things. "Oh, don't be silly," she smiled. "I've never been so happy."

That afternoon I sat in our living room quietly pondering all I had heard and seen. Carla was busy in the kitchen, cooking and talking baby talk to Sarah. She was extremely happy. Apparently knowing what was going on in my mind, she walked out and dropped a book into my lap.

"What's this?" I asked, puzzled by the cover.

"It's called the *Wordless Book*. It's all colors. There is a message on the back page that explains the meaning. Check it out, sweetheart."

It was an odd-looking book. There were colored pages: black, gold, red, and white. There were no words on the pages. I flipped to the back page and read an explanation. The black page was man's life without God—sinful and ugly. The gold page represented God's purity and holiness. The red page signified the blood of Jesus Christ that takes away our sin. And the white page represented a person whose sins have been cleansed by the blood of Lamb. A little prayer for salvation followed.

I looked through the book once more. I remembered my awareness in church that the choice was mine. I made an inner decision and slowly spoke out loud the prayer for salvation: *"Dear God, I acknowledge that I have followed my own way and that I am sinner. I ask You to forgive me and I accept the blood of Your Son Jesus Christ as an eternal sacrifice for my sin. Please accept me into Your family and guide me all the days of my life. In Jesus' name, Amen."*

For the next few minutes I stared out of the window into the backyard. I studied our big olive tree, its branches gently swaying in the afternoon breeze. I'm not quite sure what I expected to happen; a feeling, perhaps; or maybe a heavenly voice congratulating me; or an angelic choir praising my decision to take the plunge. But the truth was that I simply felt light and happy.

A heavy load had been lifted off me. I couldn't explain it, but for the first time in my life, I felt truly free. "Carla," I called softly.

Carla came into the living room, drying a dinner plate. "What's wrong, honey?"

"Well, I did it," I said.

"You did what?" she asked.

"This." I held up the book. "I said the prayer at the end of the little book you gave me. I'm saved —isn't that what you call it? Getting saved?"

I don't know how much excitement ripples through heaven when a person comes to Christ. But if it rivals the goings-on at Rosewood Lane that second Sunday afternoon in February 1977, in the town of Paradise, California, then it must be all-out wonderful.

Carla burst into tears of joy, jumped around like a little girl, clapped her hands, and thanked our Lord for bringing her husband into God's own family.

> *I say to you that likewise there will be more joy in heaven over one sinner who repents than over ninety-nine just persons who need no repentance.*
> ~LUKE 15:7

CHAPTER 4

FAMILY OF GOD

After the spontaneous celebration of my new spiritual life, Carla seized the moment. "Let's pray for something right now," she insisted.

Usually, when she got in one of those strong moods, I would rebel, but not today. She was no longer just my wife. She was now a sister in the Lord who knew a whole lot more about what was going on than I did.

"Okay," I said. "Pray for what?"

"Let's ask the Lord to take away your desire for cigarettes. Honey, please, I hate the smell of those nasty things, especially when we kiss. It'll make kissing more romantic and you'll stay alive longer!"

"Well, sure, let's go for it," I said, trying to be brave. "But you do the praying."

Carla prayed with all her heart. And to my absolute astonishment, my craving for nicotine *instantly vanished.* I felt awe for a Creator who loves, hears, and helps us humans. To think I had lived 32 years without knowing that! Why hadn't anyone told me about this wonderful God before? And why hadn't someone told my dad, so that he could have found happiness, instead of being so tormented?

At work the next week in Sacramento, I told everyone about the change in my life. My friends laughed at first, thinking it was a joke. Then they realized I was serious. One by one the guys began to avoid me. Boy, that hurt!

I had counted on these men as my partners for life, buddies who would stick with me through thick and thin. Why couldn't they understand and be happy for me? I still loved them. Why were they acting as if I had the plague? Was it because I didn't smoke, get drunk, or cuss like a sailor anymore?

But I quit blaming them. After all, how could they understand the change I had gone through? I remembered all too well the years I had known nothing about God's love. I decided to ease up. I would still be their friend and see if they would come around. Why couldn't we still go hunting and fishing together, and have a good time?

A short time later we were all working on a job near Calistoga. The new bumper sticker on my truck read, "Jesus loves you." During lunch break, someone mentioned the bumper sticker. One by one, my long-time friends took pot shots at my new-found faith. I tried to be a sport about it, but it really hurt. Why all the antagonism?

That evening, as I drove back across the valley toward Paradise, I came to a conclusion. Things would never be the same. I had to return to my old way of life to please my friends, or go all the way with Jesus and lose them. There wasn't room for compromise.

I had many fond memories of my friends, my carefree way of living, and all that went with it. But none of that compared to the new life in Christ I had found. Though I had broken more than a few promises with no sense of guilt, I wanted to keep the promise I had made to God the night He miraculously healed Carla. I had no idea what His plans were for me, but I decided to find out.

Two elderly gentlemen came to our home to talk about joining the church. Fired up by my recent decision, I jumped in with both feet. The next Sunday when the pastor gave an altar call, I walked down the aisle and made a public commitment to follow Jesus.

Afterwards, the associate pastor took me into the counseling room and asked me a strange question. "Dick, where is Jesus now?"

"In heaven," I replied, trying to sound correct.

"Yes, that is true," the minister said with a smile. "But where is He in Dick Bernal's life?"

"Oh, uh, in my heart," I answered, desperately wanting to say the right thing.

The man nodded, apparently satisfied. At the end of the counseling session, I went to ask the pastor a question. I was guarded about my secret covenant with the Lord over Carla's ordeal, so I phrased my question this way: "Sir, I feel God wants me to do something for Him. But you see, I have a, well, interesting past. I haven't exactly lived according to the Bible. You might even say I was a real sinner, if you get my drift."

Sensing my struggle to bare my soul, the minister reached for his Bible and found a passage. "Dick, listen to this," he said: *"Therefore if any man is in Christ, he is a new creature; old things passed away; behold, new things have come"* (II Corinthians 5:17). Then he asked me to read the passage back to him. I did so.

"This is God's Word, Dick," he continued. "God's Word is truth. God's Word is His will, and God says you don't have a sinful past anymore, only a glorious future. You can do anything God asks of you if you are willing."

I left the session practically glowing. On the way home, I contemplated our conversation. *Can this be true?* I wondered. *Are all those ugly, selfish things I did forgotten because of the blood of Jesus? Did God take a heavenly eraser and wipe out the sins of my youth? Am I completely forgiven for all the people I hurt and used? Boy, I want to believe this, but it seems too good to be true!*

～

The church bulletin mentioned a clean-up day the following Saturday. I thought maybe I could contribute something as a skilled construction worker and crew foreman. That Saturday at 8:00 a.m., I was the first one there, work clothes on and coffee in hand. A man with a smile on his face approached me. He held out his hand, shook mine, and introduced himself as Bill.

"Who do we have here?" he asked.

"I'm Dick," I said. "I'm new at church."

"Have you come to work?" he asked.

"Yes, sir. I'm reporting for duty. What are we doing today?"

"Oh, just the general things, you know. Cleaning up, pulling weeds, a little painting here and there, and a little roof repair."

"I'm pretty handy," I said.

Bill disappeared into the shed and came back with a large broom. "Here's a good place to start. We need the sidewalk swept."

The sidewalk swept? I said to myself. So there I was, sweeping the sidewalk for Jesus.

I was halfway done when I heard a familiar honk from an old pickup. My fishing buddy, Jim, was heading down to the local tavern for a few beers and a little pool.

He pulled over and stuck his head out the window. "Hey, Dick, what are you doing? Serving time?"

"No," I said, "Just helping out a little."

"Helping out? Hey, forget that nonsense. Let's go have some fun!"

"No thanks, Jim," I said. "There's more to be done here at the church."

He stared at me for a moment, shook his head, and drove on. I saw him crane his neck to peer at me in the rear view mirror. Does he think I'm nuts?

A little later, the tough-looking man who had greeted me at the church walked up. "Hey, Dick, you ready for a little refreshment?"

"Sure," I said, picturing the beers that Jim had offered. "What'll it be?" the man offered. "Tea or lemonade?" *Tea or lemonade,* I thought. *My gosh, what had I gotten myself into?*

But it wasn't long before Carla and I began to really like our new church home. We attended a *Young Marrieds' Class* every Sunday morning before the service. On Tuesday nights, we enjoyed a home Bible study with five other couples. The sting of rejection I felt from my former friends was eased by the care and concern of my new church family, the family of God.

> *I will be a Father to you, and you shall be my sons and daughters, says the Lord Almighty.* ~2 CORINTHIANS 6:18

A RAW & UNBRIDLED WITNESS

One Sunday morning after the service, Pastor Bob, who was

in charge of visitation, asked if I would like to learn how to witness.

"Witness?" I asked. "You mean talking to people about God? I don't think I'm quite ready for that, Pastor Bob."

The next day at work, I tried to picture myself witnessing and talking to people about the Lord. It might not be all that hard if only I knew what to say. The following night Carla and I showed up at the *Evangelism and Visitation* class. Pastor Bob taught from a little yellow booklet called the *Four Spiritual Laws*. The principles he discussed made sense to me and seemed simple enough to share with others.

Bob separated us into teams of two, pairing seasoned veterans with newcomers. Then he told each team to visit a family who had attended our church for the first time. After a word of prayer from our fearless leader, we all left with assignments in hand.

My cohort gently knocked on the door of an attractive split level home. When I heard footsteps, I took a half-step backward. I didn't feel all that confident.

The door jerked open and a man eyed us suspiciously. "What do you want?" he bellowed. I noticed a highball in the man's hand and smelled whiskey in the air.

"Hello, sir," replied my associate. "We're from the church you attended last week. May we come in and talk to you about Jesus?"

"Ethel, come here," the man yelled.

Poor Ethel came to the door. It was obvious that she, too, had partaken of more than her share of alcoholic libation. Then old "red eyes" barked at her.

"I told you not to fill out that stupid card at the church! Now look. Here they are on the doorstep!"

"Calm down, dear," pleaded Ethel. "These nice men are just trying to do their job."

"I want to tell you two something," her husband declared. "I liked your church until that phony-baloney, silver-tongued car salesman started all that garbage about salvation. Then I wanted to vomit," he roared.

His face got as red as his eyes, and he began poking me in the chest. The more he raised his voice, the more I forgot why we were there. Here I was trying to be longsuffering as befitted a Christian. But the man got louder and uglier by the second. Suddenly, my patience snapped like a twig.

I grabbed him by the throat and dragged him out on the front lawn, intending to pound him to a pulp. Ethel was screaming her head off for the police. When my partner tried to pull me off of the man, I threatened him and Ethel both.

When the man started gagging in my arms, it dawned on me that I was choking the man I had come to save. I let go of him and ran to the car, crying, "Oh, Jesus, what have I done?" I broke into tears, knowing I'd really blown it. Certainly now God would throw me out of His kingdom. I hadn't changed at all. I was the same old Dick Bernal.

A wave of despair flooded my soul. *God, I can't live this life,* I prayed. *I'm sorry, but I'm just not cut out to be a Christian.* My partner didn't say a word as he drove us back to the church. I was dreading facing the pastor. He had placed a lot of faith in me. And Carla would be so embarrassed. I died a thousand deaths as we turned into the church parking lot.

Looking around, I thought, *Great! Everyone else is already back.*

My teammate took the pastor off to one side and began whispering to him. Carla was all smiles as her partner reported that they had led a woman to God. The other teams congratulated Carla for a job well done.

My wife then looked at me. "How did you do, honey?"

"You don't want to know, believe me," I whispered.

"Why? What's wrong?"

Just then the pastor walked up. "I tell you what, Dick," he said, "next week how about you working with me?"

"Next week?" I asked, feeling my eyes moisten with tears. "You mean you want me to come back?"

"Sure," he said. "One little setback can't stop the work of the Lord, now can it, Dick? Go on home. Everything is going to be fine. See you Sunday at church."

Pastor Bob's love and understanding kept me in the church. During the next few months, I begged God to forgive me so many times that I'm sure He got weary of my pleas. I hope that some loving believer has repaired the damage I caused to poor Ethel and her husband.

Because of ignorance or lack of discipline, baby Christians can be dangerous. Yet I found out that there is room for Dick Bernal in the kingdom of God.

> *If we confess our sins, He is faithful and just to forgive us our sins and to cleanse us from all unrighteousness.* ~1 JOHN 1:9

ANAHEIM BELIEVER'S CONVENTION

Over the next year and a half, Carla and I became fixtures

around the church. We attended barbecues, volleyball games, young-married get-togethers, and church services. I really looked forward to our home group meeting every Tuesday night. Even though most of the groups were retired folks, I grew attached to each of them. I even worked up short teachings on the Bible. But Carla began to get that far away, hungry look again.

Work was slow during the summer of 1978, so I spent more time at home. Carla kept talking about a couple of Bible teachers on the local Christian radio station.

"Honey, you have to listen to these guys. Please listen! They really are wonderful, and each program is only fifteen minutes long."

I finally gave in, wondering what could they tell me that I hadn't already heard. The speaker on the first program talked about authority the Christian has in the name of Jesus. He spoke of healing and casting out demons as if both should be available to believers today. I was interested in the message.

We sat and listened to another 15-minute program by a preacher interviewing a farmer from Arkansas about how faith could be used in hunting and fishing. *I like these guys!* I thought. They made the point that a believer should use faith in every aspect of life.

Listening to these preachers became a daily habit. They had a way of presenting the Word in a very practical fashion. I grew to cherish those little fifteen-minute broadcasts Monday through Friday.

That August, they announced an upcoming convention in Anaheim, California. We decided to take the week off and see for ourselves what that "faith business" was all about.

When we entered the conference center, I was shocked to see more than 4,000 people standing with their hands raised in praise to the Lord. We sat down in seats located behind the speaker.

As I looked around at the huge crowd, I found myself going into a trance. I had a vision, seeing myself standing before even bigger crowds and preaching the gospel. The vision gave way to an inner voice that said, *"You will certainly stand in front of bigger crowds and preach My name."*

Returning to what was going on around me, I noticed that people were swaying back and forth, singing in a foreign language I had never heard before. I remembered the day my friends and I had gotten spooked when we snuck into a "holy rollers" meeting back in Watsonville. The singing continued for several minutes. I was shocked to see Carla joining right in with these lunatics! There she stood with her hands raised and eyes closed, with what sounded to me like gibberish coming from her lips.

She had mentioned experiencing the baptism of the Holy Spirit, but I had never heard her pray in tongues before. *Who needs all this, anyway?* I thought. *Why don't they just sing regular hymns and pray in English?*

Finally, one of the preachers came out and began expounding on *Ephesians*. He shouted, jumped up and down, and even stuck his tongue out in a "raspberry" at those caught in religious traditions.

He is really quite funny, I thought. And I admitted to myself that he was effective in his point that believers needed all the faith they could muster. Towards the end of the service, he asked if anyone needed hands laid on them for healing.

Hands laid on them? Does he mean like in the Bible? Does this guy think he is Jesus or something? We don't lay hands on people in our church. What is the purpose in that anyway?

Hundreds of people streamed toward the front of the auditorium. There were so many that the ushers lined them up around the walls of the huge room. The preacher paused to announce that the Lord had just spoken to him about a particular infirmity.

Oh, wonderful! I thought. *Now God is talking to this guy in person. No wonder my pastors warned me about Pentecostals.*

"God wants to heal people here with heart problems!" declared the preacher.

"Go on, honey, get prayed for," Carla begged.

"Shhh, I'm fine, sweetheart, really. There's no problem with me. I'm okay." But she was well aware of the history of the Bernal men: heart attacks took my father and his brother, Harry, early in life. And I suffered from occasional dizziness and heart palpitations.

"Please go on up there," she pressed. "What can it hurt?"

SPIRIT BAPTISM, *"YOU'VE GOT IT!"*

Seeing I wasn't going to win this one with Carla, and fascinated by it all, I found a place and squeezed in line. As I stood there, I saw people falling over backwards. Ushers would stand behind and catch them, easing them to the carpet.

How come they're falling? I asked myself. *He's not hitting them. He's just touching their foreheads. Is this the power of God at work?*

Before I knew it the preacher was next to me. "Be healed, in Jesus' name," he shouted as he touched the person directly in front of me. I wondered if he had ever watched Oral Roberts on television years ago as I had. Just then, I felt his hand on my forehead.

Instantly, I felt as if the top of my head opened up and a breath of cool air was flowing into my body. I glanced up to see if an air conditioner had been turned on above me. Then I realized the feeling was inside my body, not outside. *How odd.* I made my way back to my seat, my body feeling light and airy.

"What did he say?" asked Carla. "What did you feel?"

Before I could answer, the song leader asked everyone to stand and worship the Lord. Nearly every person in the room lifted their hands and began to sing in the Spirit, as they called it.

Feeling left out, I thought, *Oh, what the heck! Go ahead, Bernal, lift your hands, a little bit anyway. It's not going to kill you. Besides, no one from our church is here to see you.*

I bravely lifted my arms a few inches, feeling as if weights of self-consciousness were attached to them. As everyone around me was spontaneously praising the Lord, I opened my mouth and gibberish came out! I tried again with the same result. It sounded like baby talk. I began to laugh at my dilemma. Carla asked what was wrong.

"Every time I try to praise God in English, I can't!" I complained.

"You've got it!" she screamed.

"Got what?"

"Honey, you've received the baptism of the Holy Spirit and

your new prayer language. You can speak in tongues now."

"Wait a minute," I said. "I'm not sure I want this. I didn't ask for it. What is my church going to think? Me, a tongue-talker?" But nothing could take away my wife's joy.

That night and the next morning Carla put her ear on my chest to listen to my heart. The irregularity of the heartbeat was gone. The rhythm was strong and normal. A physical confirmed the healing that had occurred. Since that summer of 1978, my heartbeat has been absolutely perfect.

As we drove home to Paradise from the Charismatic Convention, I knew somehow that our lives would never be the same.

Soon after, Carla located a small group of Charismatics who met at two o'clock each Sunday afternoon. Charismatics are Christians who believe that God still does miracles through the power of the Holy Spirit and the Word of God. Whether they are called Charismatics or Pentecostal, these believers attest to the presence of healing, visions, prophecy, spiritual gifts, and praying in tongues in the Body of Christ today.

The leader of the group Carla found was a former Roman Catholic priest named Vincent O'Shaughnessy. The church was *Paradise Christian Center.*

As much as Carla loved our own church and all the new friends we had made, she felt inwardly prompted to become involved in Paradise Christian Center. However, there was one major block—me!

I was not about to leave our first church.

> *For he who speaks in a tongue does not speak to*
> *men but to God, for no one understands him;*

however, in the spirit he speaks mysteries. ~1
CORINTHIANS 14:2

❧ MISSION TO THE FUTURE

On the second Sunday of October 1978, Northern California was enjoying a beautiful Indian summer. After church, Carla started in on me again. "Please, sweetheart, come with me to hear Pastor Vince tonight," she begged. "You'll love his teaching. He's talking about the gifts of the Spirit."

I don't know if it was the glorious weather, or the fact that the OAKLAND RAIDERS had won that day, or the knowledge that duck season was only a week away, but I was in a very good mood. "Sure, why not?" I agreed. "Let's go."

Walking up the steps to the church doors, we could hear music and singing. The pastor stood by the door greeting late-comers. "Hi, Carla, and this must be Dick," smiled the friendly man of God.

A slight Irish brogue complimented his warm manner and distinguished looks. Once everyone was seated, the pastor began teaching. I counted about twenty people. I felt sorry for them, reasoning that it must be hard to start a church with no help from a denomination. But they seemed happy and full of love.

Bernal, turn off your brain and listen to what the man has to say. You might learn something.

"This evening," he said, "I am going to talk about why you should speak in tongues."

Carla glanced at me with one of those wifely looks that says, "Boy, do you ever need to hear this!"

I had decided not to pursue my brief experience of praying in tongues at the Anaheim Convention. Praying in tongues wasn't accepted in our denomination. Looking back, I believe that I was quenching the Holy Spirit.

Now as Pastor Vince was speaking, I noticed that everything he said was backed up with Scripture. For the next hour, Pastor Vince threaded together a scriptural precedence for the gifts of the Holy Spirit—healing, visions, prophesy, singing and praying in tongues. He drew from ISAIAH, ACTS, and CORINTHIANS. I like the continuity of the Old and New Testaments. He concluded that the signs and wonders of the first century are still available for believers today.

I was amazed that the Word of God so clearly spoke of spiritual gifts as instrumental in building up the body of Christ and overcoming the powers of darkness.

As he brought the message to a close, Pastor Vince paused for a moment as if hearing an unseen voice. Then he said, "I believe someone here needs God's power in his life, someone needs the baptism of the Holy Spirit."

Dear Lord, he was looking right at me!

"Yes, praise God!" Carla shouted loudly. "Amen."

There she goes again, I thought, *answering for me.* But at that moment an inner voice echoed her sentiment. "Yes, Dick, Pastor Vince is talking about you. You need more of My power in your life. You need to receive all that I have for you."

Hesitantly, I stood up and walked forward to the altar. Before I knew it, I was surrounded by other men who laid their hands on my shoulders and prayed for me. I felt deeply supported in my quest to draw closer to God.

"Dick, relax and let God move through you," coached

Pastor Vince. "Let this happen easily. Give the Holy Spirit your vocal cords."

A quiet flow of power from within began to fill my mouth. People prayed softly for me. I could hear Carla weeping tears of' joy. I took a deep breath and exhaled. A rush of foreign words and sounds came streaming out of me. I sounded as if I were speaking on Oriental language. I raised my hands in praise and laughed with joy.

What do you know, I thought. *I can do it! I am not making this up—I feel the power of God flowing through me!*

Needless to say, the people in that little church got real happy that Indian summer night. After we got home, Carla and I stayed up until dawn, praying out loud, laughing at my strange new prayer language, and loving this awesome God of ours. My faith felt turbocharged.

The next morning, tired and blurry-eyed, I drove down the hill toward Sacramento. *"Dick,"* said a voice so clearly that it startled me, *"prepare yourself for service, for I have called you."*

"Who said that?" I asked out loud. *Was that me? Boy, I should have gotten some sleep last night. I am hearing things!*

"Lord, is that you?" I asked.

The voice came again, repeating, *"Dick, prepare yourself for service, for I have called you."* I could not tell if the voice was audible or coming from deep within me.

"Okay, Lord, you've got me," I answered. "Let's get on with it." My willingness to obey surprised me. For the first time in my life, and with a confidence that I still find incredible to believe, I had a mission to the future.

But you shall receive power when the Holy Spirit has come upon you; and you shall be witnesses to Me in Jerusalem, and in all Judea and Samaria, and to the end of the earth. ~ACTS 1:8

PART TWO

ESTABLISHING THE KINGDOM

But seek first the kingdom of God

and His righteousness,

and all these things shall be added to you.

-Matthew 6:33

CHAPTER 5

MIDWEST ADVENTURE

It didn't take me long to figure out that if God was going to use me, I needed training.

After a good deal of prayer, Carla and I decided to attend a Bible College in Tulsa, Oklahoma. Could I give up the security of my union job as an ironworker? Would we starve to death, or was God truly guiding us into a new phase of life and ministry?

God encouraged this drastic change by giving me an unforgettable dream. In it I was standing inside a huge building with a red-tiled roof, preaching to thousands of people in San Jose, California. My family and friends were in the congregation. It was a wild, vivid scene. Carla interpreted the dream as a prophetic vision that would surely come true.

The doors quickly opened for us to leave California. We rented our house to a nice family, and gave away most of our belongings, even my boat and most of my precious sporting goods. Giving my dog away brought a lump to my throat, but we could not take him with us. *Trouble* would be much happier hunting birds with my friends from work.

Saying good-bye to friends and family, we packed all of our earthly belongings inside the little station wagon, and headed off for our Midwest adventure.

After a couple of days we pulled up to the home of Carla's Aunt in Tulsa. When I stepped out into the 90-degree evening air, reality settled in. Summer in Tulsa could be miserable especially if you are not used to the humidity. *Man,* I thought, *I'm already getting homesick for the cool mountain air of Paradise.*

The next day we visited a friend's sister and brother-in-law. Richard Cardoza had just graduated from the Bible School we'd enrolled in, so he and his wife Corrine gave us the low-down on school life. We bombarded them with dozens of questions about the strange new environment. That Sunday, they took us to a church that showed me how traditional my church had been in California.

My pastors in California were silver-haired, middle-aged, and soft-spoken. These two pastors were cut from a different cloth! One looked as if he could play linebacker for the RAIDERS, and his associate reminded me of a young *Conway Twitty.* The service was alive with enthusiasm. Carla and I watched how God used these two preachers in supernatural ways. We decided to make this our new church home while in Tulsa.

During the church service, a missionary was raising money for a gospel tent to be used in India. We were pinching pennies until I could find work, but I could not resist the prompting to give $100.00 to help those missionaries buy the tent. India had always fascinated me. Now I had an opportunity to bless that nation. Little did I know that three years later, I would preach in GUNTUR, INDIA under the very tent I had helped to purchase!

That week we moved into a nice, affordable apartment six miles from campus. During the first few days of school I realized how out of shape I was academically. I had never been very good at reading, studying, and taking notes. My prayer life greatly intensified!

We used what money we had to furnish our little apartment and make the down payment on our tuition. I felt awkward after 13 years of steady employment as an ironworker to be scanning the *Help Wanted* ads. School hours were from 8:00 a.m. until noon. My only alternatives for working were swing or night shifts.

My first week of job hunting proved futile. I was overqualified for most positions. The second week found us with $12.00 to our name, after rent and groceries. Driving home from another job rejection, I felt like my chest was in the grip of a giant vise. I pulled over to the side of the road and cried out to God for help.

I walked into our apartment still feeling raw. "Sit down honey," insisted my wife. "Are you ready for some news?"

"What, dear?" "It better be good news. I've had a really bad morning."

"Well, I'm pregnant," smiled my wife.

Pregnant! God! How could you let this happen to me now? I cried out inside.

A little voice deep within whispered, "Son, you reap what you sow."

Yeah, Lord, I know, but what about the timing? Here I sit with less than $12.00 in my wallet. Bible school bills are piling up, the rent is coming due, and my wife is pregnant.

When I grumbled about our finances, my eternally optimistic wife assured me that according to MATTHEW 6:33, God would take care of us. *"Seek first the kingdom of God and His righteousness, and all these things shall be added to you."*

I thought, *I hate it when she quotes the Word to me just*

when I want to wallow in self-pity. It kind of takes the fun out of it.

The next afternoon I got in the car and prayed, "God, I'll do anything. Just get me a job, please."

The Lord took me at my word. He got me work in a convenience store.

"Mr. Bernal," said the manager, "you can start tomorrow night. Your hours are from 11:00 p.m. to 7:00 a.m. Starting pay is $3.99 an hour. If you work hard, you'll get a 15-cent raise in 90 days. Here is your shirt, a large size should do the trick."

If my friends could see me now in my cute little orange shirt, they would fall over laughing. I am either called of God or one crazy fool.

Over the next months, life consisted of school, homework, church, and sleeping now and then. Just to get by, I worked overtime 20 to 30 hours a week.

BEWILDERED BY MY PAST

I found myself getting self-conscious when Carla and I tried to fellowship with our new friends. Too often the conversation would drift around to awkward personal topics. "How many kids do you have?" "Where did you meet?" "Are your parents in ministry?" Everyone seemed to assume that this was my first marriage and that I had come from a fine Christian home – Wrong!

I felt like a second class Christian, ashamed that I couldn't speak of a wonderful childhood with God-fearing parents. If I had been totally honest, I would have said, "Oh, Carla and I have two children. I have another son back home with my ex-wife. My dad was a drunk and a womanizer. I've done my fair share of drinking, drugging, and fighting."

But over time I have come to understand that many who love and serve God, both in Biblical times and today, are chosen by Him precisely because of their human flaws and needs.

Even though I felt like a fish out of water, I knew Carla and I were at the right place at the right time doing the right thing. Deep inside I knew that God's call on our lives was based upon His grace, not upon anything I had ever done or not done.

The Christmas season came. A fellow student named Mike Behr brought us a free Christmas tree. You would have thought it was a check for a million dollars. Here we had practically nothing, yet we were filled with happiness during that Christmas.

Git-n-Go Communion

My job soon became a ministry of sorts. Working the graveyard shift gave me the opportunity to share Jesus with a lot of lonely people. I told my customers all the exciting things I was learning in school. Some were very interested, but others mocked and scoffed. A few even complained to the manager about the preacher at Git-n-Go. He called me on the carpet for witnessing.

But how could I stop telling people that their lives would he wonderful if they accepted Jesus as Lord? One night I was talking to my little congregation of regulars: two homosexuals from the porno shop, a biker's girlfriend with tattoos on both arms, a truck driver, and a bag lady. After preaching to them about how Christ died for their sins so that they could enter the kingdom of God, I led them all in the sinner's prayer. Then I had a zany idea.

"Hey, let's have communion," I said.

"Sure!" they chorused.

"Grab that grape juice on the shelf and a box of saltine crackers," I instructed them. "I'll put it on my tab."

What a sight. My first congregation! I used styrofoam cups to pass around the symbolic blood of Christ, shed for the remission of our sins. And I gave each person a saltine cracker, representing the Body of Christ, broken so that they could receive eternal life. I understood as never before that God is reaching out to all people, that Jesus came into the world not to condemn us, but that the world through Him might be saved. I'll never forget the tears in the truck driver's eyes as he reached out with a grimy hand and tenderly received the bread of life.

> *And Jesus said to them, I am the bread of life. He who comes to Me shall never hunger, and he who believes in Me shall never thirst.* ~JOHN 6:35

THE STORK BRINGS *JESSE DANIEL*

By April, Carla was eight months pregnant. Her parents were visiting us for the weekend, when a spring storm with tornado warnings moved in from the south. The crack of lightning and the boom of thunder periodically interrupted our conversation in the living room. As the afternoon wore on, Carla felt increasingly uncomfortable.

"Could it be time for the baby?" asked her mother.

The baby was not due for five weeks. But when Carla's

abdominal pains intensified, she agreed to let me take her to the hospital 25 miles away.

"Pray, Mom," she yelled as we took off. "Honey, the pains are getting real bad. Drive faster!" I put the pedal to the metal. A bolt of lightning crashed into the ground ahead of us. Carla huffed and puffed against the pains, then cried out, "The baby's almost here. Pray!"

And pray I did, like never before. Finally, we arrived. "Thank you, Jesus," I yelled as I pulled into the Collinsville Hospital parking lot.

After hurried preparations, two nurses wheeled Carla's gurney into the delivery room. Several minutes later our son was born.

"Well, he's a little early," said the doctor. "We'd better keep an eye on him for a few days, just for safety's sake."

Carla and I were so happy to have a son! Amazingly, he resembled my first son, Adam, red hair and all. "Hey, peanut," I whispered as I rocked *Jesse Daniel* in my arms. "I'm your Daddy. Welcome to the world." Then the nurse placed him back in his incubator.

I was thinking how great and merciful the Lord was for giving me a second chance to raise a son. But my euphoria was interrupted when the doctor said that Carla was hemorrhaging profusely.

"Dick, this is serious," the doctor said. "I'm going to call for help."

Carla was turning yellow from her loss of blood. Her lips were white as death, a scene all too familiar from Sarah's birth. But something new was happening to me. I was full of faith and courage. Living under the Word had developed my faith in

God's ability to triumph over Satan.

"Hey, Doc, no problem," I assured him. "Everything is going to be fine." I made a few calls to Carla's parents and friends to announce Jesse's birth.

As soon as the doctor was able to free the placenta, the bleeding stopped. He said that Carla was going to be fine.

～

Two weeks before graduation, I was cleaning up the Git-n-Go store when two rough-looking guys came in. They were acting nervous.

"Hey, guys, what's up?" I asked cheerfully.

"Give me a pack of cigarettes," the big one ordered.

"Sure, no problem," I answered. I flipped a pack up onto the counter. "That'll be 80 cents, gentlemen," I smiled.

Recently, there had been a string of robberies in the Tulsa area especially at convenience stores. In some cases the clerks were shot in the head. Something told me I was about to be robbed.

"Give me all your money," the older man demanded.

The younger one guarding the door yelled, "Hurry up and open the safe."

"I can't do that, boys." I replied. "I don't have the combination."

The older guy came around the counter to check for himself. He hit the release button on the cash register and scowled at the $80.00 he found. He stuffed the bills into his coat pocket then grabbed me. Without even thinking, I broke his grip and threw him up against the soft drink machine.

Then I caught myself. *Bernal! This guy has a gun!*

For what seemed like the longest time, we stared at each

other. I found that I was smiling at him. I figured the Lord did not send me 1,800 miles to go through Bible boot camp, just to catch a bullet in the back of the head in a convenience store. Maybe I thought I could stare him down like Davy Crockett did that old bear!

Out of nowhere a set of headlights flashed through the front windows. The older man yanked his head and yelled, "Let's split!" The thieves scrambled for the door. Had God sent the white garbage truck that pulled up in front of the store? One relieved Bible school student breathed a deep sigh of thanks to His Maker.

～

Graduation night found us all down at the Tulsa Convention Center, decked out in our red caps and gowns. We were a splendid sight. Pastor Vince had flown in from Paradise to be with us for this great night of celebration. As the diplomas were being passed out, we waited patiently for our turn.

Just before our turn came, one of the Bible School professors took the microphone and said, "We have an emergency. Would Dick and Carla Bernal please call Franklin Memorial Hospital immediately?"

My intense fear caused a ringing noise in my ears as we made our way toward the foyer. Carla kept squeezing my hand and saying, "Honey, honey," over and over, as if she were dazed. "It's okay, sweetheart, it will be fine," she repeated. "Whatever it is, it's going to be okay."

Richard Cardoza and Pastor Vince joined us in the lobby to offer support. *Man, I hate the devil for sure,* I told myself as I found the pay phone and got through to the doctor.

"Mr. Bernal, your baby sitter brought your son Jesse in here, and he is bleeding from every orifice in his little body. Can you come immediately?"

I told him it would take 20 minutes to get there. But as I hung up the phone and turned to Carla, I saw the strangest sight. She was dancing before the Lord, hands raised, a glow on her face, and praises coming from her lips.

"The Lord just spoke to me, honey," she said. "It's Jesse, isn't it? But he is going to be fine. The Lord just told me. Let's go back and get our diplomas."

"But I told the doctor we were coming right away. They'll save our diplomas. Let's go."

On the way to the hospital I recalled a vision the Lord had given me a month before. In it I was looking at the new bassinet when suddenly a large snake slithered into it. The serpent was about 20 feet long and looked quite hideous. When I came out of that vision I made intercessory prayer for Carla's health and for the well-being of our unborn child. God had forewarned me of the coming problems, yet assured me that victory would be ours.

When we arrived at the hospital emergency room, an apologetic attending physician greeted us.

"Hello, folks," said the doctor. "I am sorry to have alarmed you, but your son gave us quite a scare. Your friend Doug rushed Jesse in about an hour ago because he was bleeding from his rectum. Even his mouth and ears were seeping blood."

The doctor explained that they were having trouble stopping the bleeding, when all of a sudden it just ceased! In fact, he said it had stopped about fifteen minutes before we arrived. Later we found out that at that very moment the entire graduating class had prayed for Jesse's recovery.

Jesse was transferred to a larger hospital in Tulsa for observation. They ran some tests in an attempt to locate the source of his problem. But nothing was found. Carla shared with the doctor how God had totally healed our son.

"Well, I can't argue with that," he answered. "We can't find one thing wrong with him."

Jesse was released on a Monday, and we headed for home. California, here we come! On the way out of town we stopped by Richard and Corrine Cardoza's home to say a temporary good-bye. They were waiting for their baby to be born. Then they would come to Paradise to be with us and with Pastor Vince.

Over the next two days of driving, I couldn't help but wonder what lay ahead for us. What was my calling? Pastor? No, too many headaches and heartbreaks. Evangelist? There were enough of them already. Teacher? I liked dissecting Scriptures and explaining them to people.

Yeah, God willing, I could become a Bible teacher.

And God has appointed these in the church: first apostles, second prophets, third teachers. ~I CORINTHIANS 12:28

CHAPTER 6

GOD'S WILL, NOT MINE

Our first Sunday home, Pastor Vince asked me to share with the little congregation about our year in Oklahoma. Surprisingly, speaking from the pulpit felt natural. Vince took up an offering for us and the peoples' generosity was heart-warming. That offering was just what we needed to buy groceries and get through the first week.

While Pastor Vince wanted me to work with him, the church was actually too small to support two ministers. So, Bible school diploma and all, I called my old construction company and went back to laying iron. Any spare time was spent helping around the church and being with my family. Pastor Vince knew I needed to share what I'd learned at school or burst. He let me lead the Sunday evening services.

Around October I began feeling restless. *There is a world of people out there dying and going to hell,* I thought, *and here I am working on a bridge deck in Redding, California.*

I arrived home from work one hot miserable day and made my usual greeting, "Hey, everyone! Daddy's home."

Carla came down the hall. "Honey, guess who just called? Guess, honey!"

"It's your sisters and Ed. They want to talk to us." She explained that my brother-in-law Ed told her that he was suicidal.

"What did you tell him?" I asked."

I said, 'Praise God, Ed!'"

"You said, 'Praise God'?" I asked incredulously.

"Yes," Carla replied, "I said, 'Praise God, now Jesus can get hold of you.'"

Ed answered her, "Well, I don't know if I need Jesus, but I desperately need to talk to you and Dick."

My brother-in-law had always been one of my favorite people: successful, hard-working, and generous. Ed was a lot of fun and had a great sense of humor. But his drinking was getting the best of him. He and my sister Juanita were constantly at each other's throats. Carla told me they would be at our house at 11:00 p.m.

Ed and Juanita brought my other sister Judy with them that night. Ed was handsome in his expensive Western-style clothes. My sisters were dressed up in silk finery. Ed drove us down to the local ice cream parlor in his brand new El Dorado Cadillac. As soon as we were seated, Carla jumped right in. "Ed, you need Jesus in your life."

"I need something," Ed replied.

We shared our experience of God's love and goodness for an hour. It was getting late, so we decided to call it a night. Back in our bedroom, Carla and I prayed that Christ would enter their hearts.

We all went to dinner at a local restaurant the next evening. I was looking at the menu when the Lord spoke to me: "Go home with Ed, son. This is going to take a while."

I said, "Ed, the Lord just spoke to me about you. He told me to go home with you after we finish eating and teach you His Word."

Ed stared at me with big eyes. "Dick, if you'll come home with me and teach me the Bible, I will pay you $500.00 a week."

"Done," I answered. There are some things in life you just know are from God.

Later as I sat in Ed's home I wondered where to start. The book of JOHN? Maybe MATTHEW? —or, why not at the beginning of the Bible? Yes, I'd start with GENESIS and go from there.

After our first dinner at Ed and Juanita's home, we all gathered in the living room. I taught on creation. I could tell from their expressions that they were getting into it. Once in a while one of them would ask a question, which led to more questions. We stayed up for hours, night after night. Yet none of them were willing to commit to God with a prayer of repentance and salvation. So I just kept plugging along.

Then Lisa, my teenage niece, came down with a bad case of influenza. Juanita shared her concern about Lisa with Carla, who had been looking for a chance to demonstrate God's power to this family.

"Come on, everyone," she ordered. My brave little soldier for Christ marched us into Lisa's bedroom. With authority in her voice, she commanded the spirit of infirmity to leave Lisa, and she did not mean maybe. Both of us laid hands on Lisa's burning brow and praised the Lord in our heavenly prayer language. Within minutes Lisa's fever left her.

When Lisa sat up and said that she felt much better, Juanita and Judy looked at each other in wonderment. They became willing to receive Christ as their Savior right then, and we prayed for them with great joy.

Two sisters down, one stubborn brother-in-law to go. Instead of Ed getting closer to God, he started drinking more heavily and acting belligerently.

One night when I was praying for Ed, the Lord said, "Son, you are in a wrestling match with a demonic influence over the life of your brother-in-law. Keep persisting."

On Sunday morning we were dressing for church, when Ed stomped into the kitchen, sporting a monster hangover. "Where's the 'blankety-blank' orange juice?" he barked, jerking open the refrigerator and knocking over milk cartons and bottles. When he found there was no orange juice, he slammed the door as hard as he could. Cursing one and all, he stormed back into the bedroom.

He looks so sad, I thought. *His countenance is very dark.* I could sense a spirit of death hovering around him. Without hesitation, I followed him into the bedroom. He was buried beneath a pile of blankets and pillows as if he was trying to escape life altogether. I pulled back the covers, crawled into bed beside him, and began to weep.

Putting my arm around my poor, miserable brother-in-law, I said, "Ed, I'm not going to let you go to hell!"

Ed bolted out of bed as if he had been shot out of a cannon.

"You're right," he declared. "Let's go to church."

Amen, hallelujah, thank you, Jesus, I exclaimed silently.

After church, we all went to lunch at the Los Gatos Lodge. "Well, how did you like the service?" I asked the family. During this time I had been trying to find them a church to get plugged into so that they could get established in their faith.

"Ah, okay, I guess," Juanita answered for them. Then she said, "Why don't you start a church, Dick? We like the way you teach."

At Bible school we had heard horror stories from former pastors who were ostracized by boards of elders and deacons for even the most trivial of things. Carla and I had practically made a covenant with each other that pastoring was not for us. Forget it!

LEAP OF FAITH

Just as I was about to tell my sister that her request was impossible, that familiar voice from the depths of my being whispered a command. *"Listen to your sister. She is speaking for Me. It is My will for you to pastor right here, son."*

I gulped down the remainder of my orange juice, and reminded the Lord that my wife, who was sitting beside me, would probably divorce me, or at least shoot me, if I said yes to pioneering a work in the San Jose area. *Now, Lord, you wouldn't want to be responsible for a broken home, would you?* I asked silently.

No answer. I hate it when God does that!

I turned to Carla. "Honey, I think God wants us to, uh, start a church here."

"Yeah, I know. He told me the same thing."

A chill rippled up my spine. A church in San Jose pastored by an inarticulate ironworker who had been saved for only four years and was fresh out of Bible school seemed funny and scary at the same time. Yet what were we to do? The Lord was calling us.

One night we were driving through the Highway 680 pass, right before it dips down into the Silicon Valley. The night lights of the Bay Area shimmered before us, all the way from San Francisco to San Jose. Words from a gospel song floated out from our tape deck: "Tell them for Me, please, that I Love Them..." At the same moment, Carla and I received a shared vision of the letters "W-O-R-D" hovering like a giant rainbow over the entire peninsula. Wow! We knew what we had to do.

Back at Ed's house I agreed to become pastor of the little congregation comprised of Ed, Juanita, and Judy.

"So where do we start, Pastor Dick?" exclaimed Juanita.

She had me stumped. The Bible School didn't have a course on starting a church, and if one had been offered, I wouldn't have taken it. "Well, let's see," I said, feeling embarrassed at my ignorance. "We need a building, some chairs, a pulpit, and well, you know, church things."

Before the week was out, our congregation had grown from three people to five. Ed's daughter, Kendra, and her friend "Harley Helen," a former biker's girlfriend, had joined our ranks. What a crew! Also, Ed's three sons had been coming around a lot lately, so I thought maybe we could double our new church, if they took the bait.

Ed owned a small vacant warehouse on the east side of town. It was a bare shell, but we decided to go for it.

We broke the news to Pastor Vince up in Paradise, and he agreed to ordain me. His only sorrow was that we would no longer be a part of Paradise Christian Center.

Richard and Corrine Cardoza's baby girl had been born in July back in Tulsa. They had since moved to California. When I told them of our plans, they got excited and volunteered to help, and shortly thereafter became my associates. This was starting to sound like fun. Everyone was pulling together for the cause of Christ, with Ed's boys building a platform and pulpit for the new church.

Ron Etheridge, an old friend of Ed's, ran an office supply and gave us a great deal on 100 folding chairs. Cost did not seem to be an object to Ed, who by now was so hooked on Jesus that he wanted to do everything within his power to get this new church off the ground. To make sure of his salvation, Ed and I took a ride out into the country one afternoon and parked next to a creek bank.

"Ed," I said, "I want you to pray something with me, right now."

He nodded his head, and repeated this prayer after me:

"God, I have read in Your Word that I am a sinner who needs your grace and salvation. I accept Your Son Jesus as my Lord and Savior. I trust in Your promise that His blood was shed for me. Now please forgive my sins and give me an abundant new life. Send your Holy Spirit to help me know that this day I have been born into Your family forever. Thank you in Jesus' name. Amen."

Ed looked up at me with moist eyes. I saw a new serenity in his face. His broad smile told me that 40 years of running from God had come to an end.

OUR INAUGURAL SERVICE

Saturday night, I was so excited I couldn't sleep. Carla and *Harley* Helen were in charge of praise and worship. They practiced to *canned* music nearly all night.

The third Sunday of November 1980, saw 14 people show up for our first official church service, which included family members and Richard and Corrine, who had driven down from northern California.

The eighty-six empty chairs we put out for guests looked out of place, but we were pleased anyway. That first Sunday, I simply shared the vision Carla and I had received about bringing the Word of God to the Bay Area. I explained that if the Holy Spirit were truly behind our vision, the church would prosper and grow. I gave an altar call for salvation, rededication, and for baptism in the Holy Spirit. To my amazement, four people came forward!

I was so caught up in the blessings of the Lord that I forgot to take an offering. Juanita began waving her checkbook back and forth to remind me. We were so unprepared to take the offering that my brother-in-law Ed had to take off his cowboy hat and pass it around because we didn't have offering buckets on hand. We literally had to 'pass the hat' as it were. Our first offering was $125.00, and we were thrilled.

After the service an elderly woman came up to me and grabbed my shirt insisting that I go home with her to pray for Pete to raise him from the dead because he had passed away the night before. *Raise Pete from the dead, they didn't teach me about stuff like this in Bible School,* I thought. Offering my condolences to her, she quickly responded saying she would have none of it; she wanted a miracle. "I know you have faith to raise him up, you went to Rhema," she demanded. Donning my new pastoral counseling hat, I asked her how long she had been married to Pete and she said, "Married! —Pete's my parakeet!" She was sincere and I couldn't find it in my heart to make light of her situation so I prayed with her that day, encouraging her that Pete was probably in heaven now. This elderly woman was one of our first visitors in the history of our brand new church and I immediately began to think, *"Raise a parakeet from the dead... Is this what church is going to be like every Sunday?"*

Boy, did we leave that service chuckling.

On Monday, a city official paid us a visit. He told us that the zoning of this industrial park did not allow for a church so we could no longer meet there.

Well, Bernal, welcome to the wonderful world of pastoring, I told myself. It had not been 24 hours since our first service, and the city already had shut us down. Now what? Well, I had a few days to find an alternate meeting place. Where should I look?

"How about a hotel?" asked Carla. "They have meeting rooms, don't they?"

Ed suggested the HYATT HOTEL down on North First Street, a place he used to hang out at, especially during "happy hour." The hotel space would cost $125.00 for the day. *Boy, that's our whole offering,* I thought, but undauntedly pressed on. We put a small ad in the newspaper announcing a non-denominational Charismatic church, featuring a hometown boy as pastor.

Sunday morning, we arrived early to set up. The family showed up all decked out in their Sunday best. But I felt very disappointed that six people from the prior week didn't show up, nor did I ever see them again.

The second Sunday my palms began to perspire as I saw our little meeting room fill up with 32 people. We were growing after all, but could I keep the attention of this ethnically diverse crowd? Some of the men were dressed in suits and ties. Had they come to test this rookie preacher's anointing?

However, I got an *amen* or two during my teaching on

Faith, and several of the couples stuck around to get acquainted after the service. That Sunday morning group formed the nucleus and the future of our church. All but one of the couples is still with us today. Most are in leadership.

I wondered if God was honoring my spontaneous obedience despite my ignorance about being a pastor.

> *Trust in the Lord with all your heart, and lean not on your own understanding; in all your ways acknowledge Him, and He shall direct your paths.* ~PROVERBS 3:5-6

GROWING PAINS

Our little church kept meeting at the Hyatt Hotel until February 1981, when it became increasingly difficult to guarantee a room every Sunday. A couple of times we had to move to a different hotel, and that created confusion as folks tried to find us. We felt it was time to find a permanent location. Also, the need to have more than just a Sunday morning service was evident. The people who were attending had an insatiable appetite for the Word of God.

Our search led us to a small, antiquated library called BRINER HALL in the little town of Campbell, a suburb of San Jose. The owner of the building used it for weddings and different types of meetings. He liked the idea of using Briner Hall for church services. He let us have the building on Wednesday nights and all day Sunday for $700.00 a month. Even though that was a lot of money back then, we believed that God would provide.

With 80 chairs on the hardwood floors, the place looked more like a church. A massive fireplace and an ornate ceiling added appeal. We began holding church at Briner Hall with our congregation of about 50 people. As more were added to our flock, Richard Cardoza decided we needed to organize a ministry of helps.

On the way to church for our first Easter service, Carla and I drove by one of the larger churches in the Bay Area, *Cathedral of Faith*. My dear friend Kenny Foreman pastors the church. We could see the hundreds of cars piling into the parking lot. The church was well known for its excellent Easter drama presentation.

I encouraged myself with words of faith. *You know, Bernal, some day you also are going to have a great work that is going to impact the whole Bay Area. Pastor Foreman has been at it for nearly 20 years, so just be patient. As the Lord has blessed him, He surely will bless you.*

We pulled into our parking lot with its six stalls. When I walked into Briner Hall, I found that 120 people had shown up for our Easter service! I taught from God's Word with all my heart. During the altar call ten people came and gave their hearts to Jesus.

After the service, a couple of well-dressed young men approached me. They introduced themselves as Robert and Lynn, and said they were in the computer industry. They were investors in one of the new start-up computer companies here in Silicon Valley.

Robert and Lynn said they liked what they saw and heard in our services. They asked if they could help us financially. Richard and I met with them the next week. At that meeting they expressed how they both felt sent by the Lord to help our fledgling church. These two men gave us the financial boost we needed.

It didn't take long to realize that Briner Hall would only be temporary. There was very little parking, no air-conditioning or heating, and a fire station was across the street. When listening to the old tapes from the Briner Hall days, the sound of the sirens is very distinct. When a fire broke out somewhere, we would have to stop the service and let the trucks clear the station before we started up again. We used to laugh and blame the devil that every time I had a good message, a fire would break out.

And we needed something with facilities for children as more families were beginning to attend. Visiting a YMCA building near Cupertino on the west side of town, we found facilities that suited us perfectly.

"How many people does it hold?" I asked the man in charge.

"Oh, you can get about 300 people in the main room," he said.

Three hundred people! I thought. *Are there that many people in the Bay Area who would want to come and hear me teach? Well, we'll just have to wait and see.*

We agreed on the price of $2,000.00 a month to have the premises from Friday noon through Sunday night. That first Sunday, September 6, 1981, about 90 people came. I felt astounded by the wide range of ages, ethnic groups, and economic backgrounds. From infants to eighty-year-olds; including African-American, Hispanic, Asian, and Anglo; millionaires and street people too. The Lord was calling them one and all. I remembered reading how during the first Pentecostal out-pouring of the 20th century at the Azusa Street revival in Los Angeles, one of the most remarkable fruits of the Holy Spirit was the lack of racial prejudice. Now almost 80 years later the same thing was happening before my eyes.

DON'T BEAT THE SHEEP

Looking back over the first full year of pastoring, it amazes me that the foolish things I attempted didn't sink the whole ship. I really panicked during the first summer of slumped attendance, even though this phenomenon plagues most churches. Richard and I had been going out on Saturdays witnessing and inviting people to our new church. Dear Lord, we met every conceivable type: burned-out druggies, flipped-out Vietnam vets, fast-living bikers, lonely housewives, and friendly senior citizens.

I had just read a book on soul winning, and it set me on fire. Carla and I would go to shopping centers between Sunday services, pass out tracts, and invite folks to the evening service that usually averaged about 10 people. I was determined to see the church grow.

One Sunday in July, I decided to straighten out the congregation. "Either you can go out into the highways and byways with me to witness, or you can find another church," I told them. I felt righteous as I lambasted the crowd of 75 for their apparent lack of concern for the lost. I shouted, whooped, and hollered about the wages of slothfulness. I told them to show up next Saturday at church for their neighborhood witnessing assignments.

On Saturday, I drove up fully expecting an army of zealots. Instead, there was Richard, a young man named Scott, a young girl, and me. Then I really got indignant. "If they thought last Sunday was scathing, just wait until tomorrow," I threatened. "I'm going to pin their ears back for good. Just wait and see."

The next morning I drove to church feeling like a fiery prophet sent by God. I pulled into a near empty parking lot. "Where, are all the cars?" I asked Carla.

"You probably scared them off last week, honey," she gently replied.

"What? No way! They needed a little shaking up. They'll be here, won't they?"

At 10:00 a.m., Bill hit a few chords on his guitar and began leading the people in praise and worship. I counted ... 26, 27, 28 in attendance. I was still counting heads when I should have been worshipping God. At 10:30, the announcements were read from the church bulletin. No one else showed up. Carla's words rang in my ears.

That summer setback cost us over half the congregation. Instead of beating the sheep again, I changed my message to one more suitable for new babes in Christ. I worked on tempering my brazenness with patience and love.

Not everyone is a *Philip* or a *Paul*. Many never will be. I prayed for the Holy Spirit to help me become more accepting of the people as God is.

> *But the fruit of the Spirit is love, joy, peace, long-suffering, kindness, goodness, faithfulness, gentleness, self-control.* ~GALATIANS 5:22-23

A COLOSSAL BLUNDER

Richard and Corrine felt that God was leading them back to northern California to pioneer a church. We prayed for God to bless them, but I really felt the loss of my associate and confidant.

By now I was on full salary, relieving my brother-in-law of his commitment of $500.00 a week. We still had fewer than 100 members. My two young computer entrepreneurs told me that money was no object. They encouraged me to hire a new assistant.

About that time, one of my members introduced me to a young preacher who had just left a small church across town. Apparently he and the senior pastor had come into conflict over financial matters.

This out-of-work pastor was introduced to me Sunday morning. That night he and his wife returned for the evening worship service and joined us for coffee afterwards. I took a liking to him and asked if he would like to work with me. I even dangled a salary and title in front of him. He said he would discuss it with his wife and get back to me in the morning.

On the way home, Carla said, "Honey, why did you offer that man a job? We don't know a thing about him, his background, his doctrine, or anything."

"Oh, Carla, relax! He's okay," I reassured her. "I like him and I like his wife."

"That's not the point, dear," she retorted. "I like him too, but is he right for our church? Will he flow with our vision? You wouldn't marry someone after a first date, would you?"

"Carla, stop being so paranoid. This is different."

"Did you pray about it?" she asked.

I really hate it when she does that!

"Give me a break!" I complained. "I'm not totally helpless. God probably gets tired of me always bugging him with questions. I'm a big boy with a good head on my shoulders. Trust me, dear."

However, after a few months of trying to make our association work out, I could see that I had made a big mistake. The chemistry between us was wrong. Our different personalities made it impossible to pull together as a team. A couple of years later this associate took several of our congregation to start his own church across town. But his church folded in six months because of his antagonistic pulpit style. This underscored to me that a pastor's personality plays an important role in the spiritual health of his ministry.

I also learned that a pastor who does not diligently seek the Lord before hiring key staff people must bear the pain when things backfire. Successful pastors have shared with me this important truth - your staff will make or break the church.

Pray without ceasing. ~1 THESSALONIANS 5:17

CHAPTER 7

PASSAGE TO INDIA, AND BEYOND

By Christmas of 1981 our church had leveled off at about 120 people attending the Sunday morning services. I thanked God for the progress we had made, but wondered if the church had peaked.

But my bigger question was, why couldn't we keep growing and become a church of 200, or even 2,000? If God was willing - He gave His Son for our salvation and showed unlimited willingness - then how might we expand our horizons in the kingdom of God?

The Bernal family had been one of the pioneering Spanish families back in the early 1800s. They were a tough, durable lot, forging a life out of a wilderness in the name of God and king. I burned with desire to impact the land of my forefathers. I figured if my Roman Catholic ancestors had the courage to press on, their Protestant Charismatic descendents could do no less.

I was developing an insatiable interest in the dynamics of church growth by this time. Why did some churches teem with excitement and run out of room for the people, while other churches remained stuck on plateaus or downright deteriorated?

I started reading every book I could get my hands on about church growth. I would frequently attend any minister's seminar within driving distance to glean new ideas that would help our church. My old church back in Tulsa announced a conference for new pastors. I knew I had to be there. One of the young businessmen in my church offered to underwrite my trip. Maybe he knew we needed all the help we could get for our infant church.

One of the conference keynote speakers was Dr. Lester Sumrall, a statesman and veteran of overseas ministry.

Morning, noon, and night, I sat there receiving instruction, correction, and especially encouragement from all the speakers. The late Dr. Sumrall, who became one of my dearest friends before passing on to glory, laid his hands upon me and prayed for the anointing of God to go through me. Boy did I feel a jolt!

As I was leaving an afternoon session, I overheard a group of preachers talking about going to India the following February.

India! I thought. *Oh, God, can you work this out? I've just got to go to India.*

I can't honestly say God told me in so many words to go to India, but I had a strong witness in my heart that I was supposed to go on this deployment. So I walked up to the group, waited for the right moment, and piped up, "I'm interested in going to India too. What do I have to do?"

They told me to attend an afternoon meeting where different veterans of missions to India would talk about the proposed trip. I was so excited to find out more I could hardly eat lunch.

That afternoon I heard different pastors expound on the "do's and don'ts" of the mission field to a small group of us. I trembled with anticipation. They spoke about India's demons, idol worshippers, paganism, and snake charmers. *Oh, boy this is going to be fun!*

I arrived home in San Jose late Saturday night and immediately shared with Carla my new passion about going to India.

"India!" Carla yelled in bewilderment. "Why do you want to go to India?"

"I just do, honey," I said. "I believe God would have me see a part of the world I have never seen. It would do me and our church good."

"Okay," answered my concerned wife. "But I'm not sure about all this."

The next morning I announced to my congregation, "Your pastor is going on a mission to India." Riding the tide of many *"Amen's"* and *"Hallelujah's,"* I announced my need for financial help. "And I need $2,000.00 to get me there and back and to cover living expenses."

There were only about 50 people present that morning. Many began standing and making pledges in various amounts. We started counting on the spot, until at $2,700.00, I yelled, "Stop! That's enough; gee, I didn't know you wanted to get rid of me that badly."

We all laughed and rejoiced together.

TRAVELOGUE DESTINATION: *GUNTUR, INDIA*

In February 1982, I was wheels-up and in the friendly skies, departing from San Francisco International and eastbound to meet the rest of my INDIA team at New York's Kennedy Airport. We then flew across the Atlantic, with layovers in Paris, Kuwait, and other places too difficult to pronounce.

We finally landed in Bombay. I was so keyed up and full of French coffee that sleep was impossible. I had heard of culture shock and been told about India, but was not prepared for the sights, sounds, and smells of a Third World country. Aromas from exotic cooking spices, and stench from animal dung and open sewers filled the air.

Beggars jammed the streets. The poverty was overwhelming. Every now and then I'd see a cow wandering aimlessly about. Even though I'd been warned about the conditions, I could still barely comprehend what I was seeing.

"My God!" I exclaimed to one of the pastors. "Right here on our planet people are living worse than our pets do back home! Human beings, people for whom Jesus died, are living like gutter rats."

Another pastor leaned over and whispered, "I wonder if this is the result of so many people worshipping demon idols?"

I clutched my Bible, thanking Jesus for *America* and for my Christian faith. I couldn't help but picture my own children in this environment, shuddering at the thought.

Later, we caught a propeller airplane to the city of Hyderabad, near the center of India. From there, the *Krishna Express* train took us on a 7-hour journey across this mysterious yet captivating country. With all of its poverty there is a raw, stark beauty about India. In fact with all its poverty there is also raw, stark humor. Having arrived at our destination, we were awakened by a porter rapping on a coffee cup, announcing, *"Coffee, coffee, coffee."* Pouring coffee, one paying customer would drink, then the porter would pour coffee for the next customer —*into the same cup*. I decided to pass on the KRISHNA EXPRESS latte.

I noticed how kind the Indian people were, almost childlike. Peeking over the backs of their train seats at the foreigners from

America, they'd burst into giggles when we would catch them staring. We reached our destination late Wednesday afternoon, a place called GUNTUR. A large group from the Lutheran Church and Bible School greeted us and we were soon ushered to a local restaurant to try their traditional South Indian cuisine – the *tandoori* chicken, *dal* soup and fresh garlic buttered *naan* were simply delicious!

Guntur is the headquarters for the Lutheran Church in Central India. Their missionaries would host this weeklong preaching and miracle crusade. The promotional literature around town actually guaranteed miracles, signs, and wonders. I asked if I might have an opportunity to teach on the Bible. They quickly informed me that we were not here to teach but to preach to the lost – to the Hindus and Muslims in particular.

Preach? I thought with alarm. I've never preached in my life. *I'm a Bible teacher. I'm 13,000 miles from home with a suitcase full of teaching notes, and they want me to be a Billy Graham!*

As we checked into our run-down motel, I noticed the strange wallpaper. It had lizards on it. "Why would anyone want lizard wallpaper?" I asked my roommate. Then I noticed that the wallpaper was moving. Gross!

Our hosts assured us that this was the best lodging we could get. Reluctantly, I flopped down on my rock-hard bed. A short while later a knock woke me out of a deep sleep. I answered the door feeling like a zombie.

One of our hosts told me that a meeting was taking place right away. Attendance was mandatory. A meeting! The last thing I wanted to do was go to a meeting.

At the meeting I learned to my utter dismay that I was to

preach that night in a town 40 miles away, whose name I still cannot pronounce. Apparently, our hosts had set up satellite meetings in several surrounding villages to promote the big crusade that would start in a few days in Guntur. My missionary zeal rapidly waned. I suddenly craved a hug from my wife, a square meal, and my own bed back home. But I brushed off my travel worn clothes and dashed out the door.

"ME PREACH TWO HOURS?"

A fellow American from Minnesota, Gayland, three Indian brothers, and I stuffed into a tiny cab and ventured out into the Indian night. A quiet settled over us as if we were commandos headed into the danger zone. Small candle-lit shrines, no larger than walk-in closets, appeared about every mile along the road. People knelt worshipping graven images. The sight gave me the creeps.

Demon worship, I told myself. I wonder if any evil spirits will manifest tonight in our meeting?

In a clipped British accent, one of the hosts turned and asked, "Reverend Dick, will you please preach for at least two hours, sir?"

Two hours? I had never before preached *two minutes.* I smiled and nodded yes to my gracious host, while wincing at the thought. Then I turned to my American associate and told him it would please the Lord if he opened the program and shared what was on his heart for "as long as he wanted."

He agreed. I hoped I had bought myself enough time to get a message together. *Oh, God,* I pleaded, *help your poor undeserving servant get out of this mess, please!*

As we pulled into the grounds, I could see thousands of beautiful brown-skinned faces staring at us. Many began to stand as we made our way to the rustic makeshift platform. Music and singing had been underway for hours and I could make out the tune of the chorus, *This Is The Day.*

After several introductions of everyone who was anyone, a custom you get used to on the mission field, Gayland, my preaching partner, was introduced to the crowd. I figured he was good for at least an hour of time. Hopefully, he might last an hour-and-a-half. Certainly I could gather at least a few thoughts on something worth preaching about from my Bible.

But after a mere 20 minutes, I heard Gayland say, *"And now, ladies and gentlemen, it gives me great pleasure to introduce to you one of America's great preachers, all the way from the San Francisco Bay Area; would you welcome Reverend Dick Bernal."*

Struggling to my feet in a daze from lack of sleep and near terror, I whispered into the microphone: "Hello, everyone."

My little Indian interpreter followed suit, even to the whisper. I cleared my throat and took a deep breath. And so did he.

Is he an interpreter or a mimic? I wondered. *Boy, these guys are really trained.*

I began by sharing my lifelong desire to visit India, but had no clue where to proceed from there. Then out of nowhere came an inner prompting to share the story of Elijah, the prophet of God, and his encounter with Ahab and the prophets of Baal on Mount Carmel. I flipped the pages of my Bible to *I Kings, Chapter 18.*

As I found the text, a strange sensation came over me. I felt as if an invisible person was pouring warm oil over my head.

The sensation eased down through my body, transforming my fatigue and fear into a wonderfully exhilarating feeling of confidence. To my astonishment, I began to preach!

> *Hear me, O Lord...that this people may know that*
> *You are the Lord God, and that You have turned*
> *their hearts back to You again...Now when all the*
> *people saw it, they fell on their faces; and they*
> *said, the Lord, He is God! The Lord, He is God!*
> ~1 KINGS 18:37,39

Within moments I was prancing around the platform, shouting and challenging all the demons of that city to come for a showdown. We would prove that night whose God was the true and everlasting God. I felt like Elijah himself. An hour rushed by, and I was just getting warmed up. Sweat dripped off me, yet I was loving every minute. *I hope they are taping this,* I thought. *My home church will never believe this!*

Before I knew it another hour had zoomed by.

"Let's pray for the sick," yelled Gayland. "Especially those with respiratory problems. The Lord has given me a word for them." "Sure," I said. "Let's do it."

I gave the invitation for people to come forward and receive Christ. I said that we would also lay hands on them for divine healing. But I was totally caught off guard when the enormous crowd bolted like a stampeded herd toward the platform where I was. I had been preaching directly in front of the platform and the ministers had to reach down and rescue me from being crushed. It took nearly fifteen minutes to establish order out of the chaos.

We finally got the people to form two long prayer lines. I looked down at my watch and it was nearly midnight. "Man, I'm pooped," I told Gayland. "Look at all these people, we're going to be here until dawn."

I was relieved to see no stretcher cases, leprosy, or deformities in my prayer line. In fact, they all looked fairly normal. Most of the people were young ladies with bright red dots on their foreheads.

"God," I prayed, "I have been bragging on you for two hours. Don't disappoint these poor, needy people. Bless them now."

I laid my hands on the first person, praying a blessing in Jesus' name and moved on to the next one. I quickly learned not to ask what was wrong, because people would tell me exactly what the doctor had said, and what their mothers, fathers, and grandparents had said. So instead I prayed for God to tailor His blessing to each need.

DEMONS CONGREGATE

I laid my hands on one young woman's head and began to bless her in the name of Jesus. She dropped to the ground as if shot, slithering like a snake and making guttural noises. Her tongue darted in and out, while her eyes bulged out at me.

I froze, *what in the world is all this?*

No one around me did a thing. She slithered over toward Gayland, and I was very thankful that he was going to have to deal with her. I decided to continue praying and ignore the interruption. But then she was back, all curled up around my feet. She glared at me tauntingly.

"Demons, Reverend Dick! Demons," my Indian friends told me.

"I know that," I assured my hosts, trying to sound like a demonology expert.

Three men picked her up and placed her in front of me. I recoiled at a demon literally looking out of her eyes at me. To cover up for my lack of training I just stared back at it. But as I attempted to pray for her, she broke free from the grip of the three men and began running for the road.

"Good riddance, lady," I murmured under my breath.

Instantly, the inner voice of the Lord commanded me, saying, *"I didn't send you here to be mocked at, but to set people free. Go get her and deliver her in front of these people."*

I had learned that when the Father speaks in that tone, obedience is mandatory. I sprinted after her, dodging between people. I caught up to this poor possessed soul and grabbed her arm. We both tumbled to the ground. She couldn't have weighed more than 90 pounds, yet she was imbued with incredible demonic strength. I tried to pin her down, but she threw me off like a rag doll. My skin crawled as it sunk in to me that I was literally wrestling a demon.

My three Indian minister friends caught up to us and began to help me. The four of us finally gained control of the girl. I used my thumbs to pry open her eyelids. An anointing from the Lord shot through me. I commanded the demon to leave in Jesus' name. It left her with a tearing sound. Her body went limp, and when she opened her eyes they looked peaceful.

We all stood up and regained our composure. When I realized that she could speak English, I led her in the sinner's prayer and had her denounce all her former idol worship. I instructed her to go home, destroy all the idols, and plead the blood of Jesus throughout her entire house.

We walked back to the two prayer lines and continued our work. About an hour later, several people brought up a Hindu priest. An old man with long white hair who wore a traditional orange robe and had his face painted like an *Apache* warrior; white and red stripes on his forehead and cheeks. His eyes were covered with milky-white cataracts. They told us he'd been blind for 8 years.

Gayland and I laid hands on his head and prayed in Christ's name for the restoration of his sight. The old man took one step forward and the white vanished from his eyes. He could see!

My mouth dropped open. *This stuff really works,* I thought. I watched as he started trembling under the power of the Holy Spirit. Tears poured down his cheeks as he turned his head looking at everyone. A pastor told me later that the old man went to a little church in NARASARAPIT and walked around with his arms raised in praise all night long, saying, "Jesus, Jesus."

I continued praying in the healing line until the wee hours of the morning. I felt utterly exhausted, yet happy as could be. God gave me enough strength to last until all the people had gone home. That morning as sunlight filtered through the windows of my hotel room, I hit the bed with a thud, feeling awe at all I had experienced.

On the remaining nights of our crusade, God continued to show evidence of His signs and wonders. On the third night one of the people in the prayer line was an English-speaking father, dressed in a white shirt and dark slacks, who had brought his seven-year-old son. He told me that his son was mute. The boy hadn't spoken in four years.

I prayed for the child, laying my hand on his forehead: "You foul demon spirit-let him loose, in Jesus' name!" Then I knelt down to him. "Say hallelujah," I coached.

The little boy looked up at me. "Hallelujah," he whispered.

His father jumped, startled. So did I. Then I said to the boy, "Say Jesus."

The boy smiled and said, "Jesus!"

His father was so beside himself with joy that he started kissing me.

"Do you have idols in your home?" I asked the young boy's father.

"Yes," he replied. "Many."

This didn't surprise me, since I had personally seen idols of gods like *Vishnu* and *Kali* in several of the homes I had visited. "Go destroy them at once," I declared. "Otherwise your child will become mute again. Now you serve the one true and living God." The simplicity of the Bible message struck me with new force: *"For this purpose the Son of God was manifested, that he might destroy the works of the devil"* (1 John 3:8).

By this time I began to feel an electrical power fill my body. I felt like there was nothing too hard for the Lord. A man weighing all of 75 pounds, all crippled up, made his way towards me on a pair of handmade crutches. Suddenly, I heard the Lord command me to kick his crutches away, grab him by the arm, and start running. Not stopping to think, I kicked both crutches out from under this poor man and started dragging him for about 30 yards while he's screaming the whole time. The Lord told me not to look at the man, but to just keep running. Finally the guy struggled up onto his legs and started running with me like a *Forrest Gump!* We ran through the crowd like track stars

- a field of faith streaming over, around, and through us. People were cheering like crazy and crying out for the Lord.

When I got back to the platform, I became aware that the whole prayer team was so empowered by the Holy Spirit that thousands were accepting the invitation for Christ. People were crying or laughing or jumping for joy as the Holy Spirit witnessed within them that they, too, were now sons and daughters of the living God. I felt as if we were working alongside *Peter* and *Paul* in the book of *Acts*.

> *Grant to Your servants that with all boldness they*
> *may speak Your word, by stretching out Your hand*
> *to heal, and that signs and wonders may be done*
> *through the name of Your holy servant Jesus.*
> ~ACTS 4:29

ENCOMPASSING A LARGER VISION

I came back from India with a bad case of diarrhea, jet lag, and fire from heaven burning in my soul. The first Sunday in my home church I felt catapulted into action, preaching and praying with unusual boldness. And there were results! The Holy Spirit moved upon people - one woman was healed of cervical cancer and many others were filled with the Spirit. In two weeks our attendance soared.

Soon our meeting room at the YMCA could barely contain the 250 adults. The children's rooms were packed. One warm Sunday in May, I looked out the sanctuary window and saw a traffic jam outside. *Is the Y sponsoring some other function?* I thought. I began my morning message, but was distracted by the head usher who was looking around frantically.

"What's up, Scott?" I asked from the pulpit.

"Pastor," he said, "people are lined up down the hall, trying get in."

I glanced out the window and cars were circling the parking lot trying to find a space to park. We stopped the service long enough to carry in chairs from an auxiliary room, squeezing in another 75 folks. I immediately announced that we would start having two services the next Sunday morning.

By the end of the summer of 1982, both services were totally filled. About 600 people, including children, were attending.

In early 1983, an opportunity came for me to start doing a radio program. I felt comfortable with radio, and pretty much preached up a storm, just the way I do in church.

"Don't ignore the power of media, it will reach more people than you can imagine," I recall Oral Roberts encouraging us in Bible School. With those words ringing in my ears, my associate and I also started searching for other inexpensive ways to reach the Bay Area when along came an invitation to purchase airtime on cable television. Boy was I excited. Sitting in front of a camera was a little intimidating at first, but I soon enjoyed the opportunities the Lord was blessing us with. I can still remember my first message broadcasted on Gill Cable, Channel 5-B – *Faith Which Works by Love*

One Sunday morning two African-American sisters attended the worship service. Afterwards, one of these dear ladies, named Cora, came up to me and said, "I listened to you on the radio and thought for sure you were a black preacher. That's why I came this morning. Now I know you're a white boy, but I still like what you say. I think I'll keep coming back." Not only did she come back, but Cora and her sister Dorothy eventually became Jubilee church mothers.

Over time, a larger influx of African-Americans came through the church doors. But their trust of a white preacher didn't come easy. I think Cora said it best. For three years she called me Dick or Mr. Bernal. Then a day came when she introduced me to one of her friends. My ears perked up when she said, "I'd like you to meet Pastor Dick." She had never called me her pastor before. And I had never taken issue about it, because a title of pastor has to be earned.

~~~

My missionary zeal was intensifying and my travels abroad were now taking me on a missionary journey with Dr. Lester Sumrall for two weeks to the Philippines, Hong Kong and Red China. This was a chance of a lifetime for me to get up close and learn from an elder statesman who was well acquainted with the demonic world. I admired him from afar and somehow felt a connection to him.

My paradigm of how church is celebrated beyond my typical American experience was beginning to change. Every culture and nation has its own way of having church, and firsthand observation was moving me outside of the traditional religious form I knew. The Filipinos, our strong American allies, know how to have church. They know how to celebrate the Lord in an exuberant style of worship; they are a very upbeat, hospitable and friendly people. Red China, on the other hand, was another story altogether, and my experience left a lasting impression on me. I was excited to visit China for the first time, but immediately became aware that we were being followed by the Secret Police. I had a feeling that we weren't going to have church like we did at home; everything we did and everywhere we went was monitored. This was all new to me, but I was eager to learn and follow my fearless leader and not become distracted. We had a few close calls, but we were wiser for our stay in China.

I saw firsthand the oppressive effects Communism has had on a nation. It is a form of godlessness that removes all color, laughter, and joy from their lives. Everything, including the people appeared to be drab and lifeless.

Disembarking the plane at San Francisco airport, the familiar sights and sounds were welcoming. Dorothy from the land of *Oz* said it well, "There's no place like home." And I sure appreciated coming home to my family, a home cooked meal, and laboring at our new fledgling church.

‿

To keep up with the growth, I hired a full-time children's pastor from Oklahoma and a personal secretary. Our home phone was ringing off the hook with inquiries about this growing Charismatic church. The annual church income had steadily climbed to almost a half-million dollars. We kept our overhead low which enabled us to bank $120,000.00.

It was obvious that the YMCA had outlived its usefulness. We needed a more permanent church home. Finding a new facility became my number-one priority, outside of prayer and study. Alan Vandermade and I scouted the whole South Bay Area with little success. The places we found were too big, too small, or too expensive. When we found places that fit our needs and pocketbook, the owners didn't want to do business with a church, especially one that was only two years old with no denominational backing.

Our two young investor friends, Robert and Lynn, came to the rescue. Robert and Lynn owned computer stock valued in excess of $20 million. Both men wanted to tithe off their stock sales in the spring of 1983, when the company they invested in was supposed to go public.

Later, Alan and I found a vacant warehouse with 40,000 square feet. The place would seat about 1,200 people. The asking price for the building and the land was $3.8 million.

Once the corporation's representative saw that we were serious and able to handle the transaction, a deal was struck. We occupied the building in March 1983, on a lease option at $40,000.00 per month. We were counting on the tithe from Robert and Lynn's stocks in early summer to bring close to $2.5 million. Then we could get the monthly payments down to a reasonable level.

Everyone was excited about our new and larger church home. Our first Sunday found 750 people in attendance with several visiting families. Kenny and Shirley Foreman, our dear friends and pastors of San Jose's Cathedral of Faith, congratulated us by sending a beautiful floral arrangement.

Rarely a service went by where five or ten people did not come forward to find Jesus or to rededicate their lives. That first Sunday more than 30 people responded to the invitation. The next Sunday was Easter, and I had a terrific message ready that I had been working on for weeks.

"I wonder how many people are here," I whispered to Carla during the pulpit announcements. Afterwards I found out that there were more than 1000 people in attendance. Imagine that! More than 50 came to the altar to get right with God after the Easter morning sermon. The ushers proudly announced that the morning tithes and offerings brought in more than $14,000.00

What was all that silly talk about the hardships of pastoring? I asked myself. *Here I am with a new building, $2.5 million only weeks away, a church growing at a rate of two hundred people a month, and invitations coming in from various places to speak.*

I had spoken too soon.

FINANCIAL GLOOM

By midsummer of 1983 the stock had still not gone public. Lynn dropped by my office one afternoon looking pale and nervous. He told me that the computer company had just filed for Chapter 11 bankruptcy. Not only were Lynn and Robert out several million dollars, but Pastor Dick was left holding a building that he and his church could not afford.

How do I tell the congregation? I thought.

I could just hear the devil gloating: "Well, big shot, maybe you can write a book on church collapse in one easy lesson. You're done, Bernal. It's over. Finished. I've got you now, boy. These people are going to abandon you and this church as soon as word gets out about how their pastor brought them to financial ruin."

I became so depressed. I refused to go to the office and would lay on the couch at home feeling sorry for myself. Even thoughts of suicide nipped my heels like rabid dogs.

My optimistic wife tried her best to cheer me up. "Oh, honey, God is our source, not some computer company."

Somehow, I was not in the mood for a Holy Spirit rally, even though I knew deep down in my heart that she was right.

Against my wishes, she called an old friend from Tulsa.

It turned out that his church in Tulsa was also in a financial crunch, so we had common ground. After a couple of hours of ministry over the phone, I was able to say to him, "Yeah, you're right. No big deal. If God is in this work, it will all come out in the wash. If not, then let it die." I'm grateful for friends to whom I can turn in times of need.

The next day, I left home encouraged but realistic. *We've got a major problem, Lord, but You're at the wheel, and I'll keep driving as long as You give me the go-ahead.*

When I got to my office, I discovered that Robert was waiting for me. For a man who had just lost several million dollars, he looked relaxed and confident. He told me he would borrow $100,000.00 to help us offset our negative cash flow. He virtually was wiped out, yet he managed to muster up funds for his church. I am happy to report that today Robert is doing just fine, as the Lord honored his sacrifice. And his generous offering gave us what the church needed to weather the financial storm.

I know how Peter must have felt when he was sinking under the waves and crying out for the Lord to keep him from drowning. Yet the real message of Peter's experience is that Jesus can turn a stunning setback into a glorious triumph for the kingdom of God. Glory to God!

> *Jesus spoke to them saying, "Be of good cheer! It is I; do not be afraid." And Peter answered Him and said, "Lord, if it is You, command me to come to You on the water." So He said, "Come." And Peter had come down out of the boat, he walked on the water to go to Jesus. But when he saw that*

the wind was boisterous, he was afraid; and
beginning to sink he cried out, saying, "Lord,
save me!" " And immediately Jesus stretched out
His hand and caught Him... ~MATTHEW 14:27-31

FACING MY LIMITATIONS

The year 1984 was one of those peak years. A new inflow of people began pouring through our doors, and most of them were staying. As our church grew, I mistakenly believed that I was supposed to jump every time a member hollered. I ran from house to house listening to all the complaints and trying my best to put out all the fires. I figured counseling was a mandatory role of the senior pastor, so I opened my door to one and all.

One day I woke up to the fact that I am not a very good counselor. I enjoy praying, fellowshipping, and teaching the saints. But counseling definitely was and is not one of my strong points. So I appointed a counseling pastor. I was learning to accept my weaknesses, while concentrating more on my true strengths. I figured that if the apostles could admit their earthly limitations, so could I.

Our praise and worship was boisterous and full of life. Carla said that my teaching and preaching skills were maturing. I was now honing my skills in television, hosting a weekly talk show program, *Zoe - The Supernatural Life* on Channel 42 and Gill Cable Channel 5-B. I was interviewing well-known Christian leaders including none other than Dr. Lester Sumrall. We would discuss topics such as Demonology, Angelology and Eschatology. I enjoyed the challenge of keeping up with these and other topics as I went along because the things I was learning intrigued me and helped me in seeing the bigger picture.

As the church began to gain notoriety at home, to my surprise many ministries began calling me so that they could come and speak at our church. I was getting acquainted with an connected to many well-known Christians in the secular arena as well as the Christian community. Many who I had the opportunity to pastor became my longtime friends. One such individual I recall in those early years was Wendell Tyler, star running back for the San Francisco 49ers who was the first of many Christian football players I would later meet.

We had the privilege of hosting Dr. Kenneth Hagin at our church in 1984 and 1986. He taught and expounded on the ABC's of faith and healing. At the time Brother Hagin had been in ministry for over 50 years and I felt privileged to host him and received much love and wisdom from this veteran of the faith during our intimate times together. Though he finished his course and passed on to glory in 2004, he never wavered from his inspirational message of faith.

$$\smile$$

By the end of 1984, we had around 1,500 members. Our income was $1.3 million. My dear colleague Richard Cardoza had returned from Eureka to help administrate the church and run our new Bible College with a 150-student enrollment. We were also running a Day Care Center and a K-3 Christian school that was filling up rapidly.

We were – *A Family Church, a World Outreach and a Charismatic Teaching Center*. True to our calling to raise up leaders to thrust them into the harvest, our Bible College began to flourish. In those early years my concept of a Bible College was to train students for the five-fold ministry – Apostle,

Prophet, Evangelist, Pastor, and Teacher. Unfortunately, training for the five-fold ministry didn't take into account the majority of the church who are not called to five-fold ministry; we also hadn't taken into account the marketplace. I believe that the Bible College's early years had its purpose, and I am grateful for the fruit that has remained. It has produced most of our church leadership, including many who are in full time ministry today, along with my son, Adam. Indeed, SOLOMON aptly spoke in Ecclesiastes that "To everything there is a season and a time under heaven...." It wasn't until the year 2000 that things changed drastically. We shifted into the G-12 vision, which empowers the laity to do the work of Jesus because it underscores that all members are potential leaders. Therefore, the Bible College became a more effective tool to implement the vision.

Other lessons I learned during this season continue to tutor me as I reflect, and encourage others with regard to our School and Day Care Center. Truthfully, the Grade School and Day Care Center were never my idea. I let well-meaning parents in the church talk me into implementing their vision, something we were ill equipped to handle. I had no idea what it took to have a successful school. Here we were a start-up church expending our energies trying to put out administrative fires, had parents who were not paying their tuition, and losing $10,000 a month. I began to realize that it was hindering the real vision of the church. We were an evangelistic, mission minded worship center and didn't even have a sanctuary to hold church. We needed to be focused on acquiring our own sanctuary and these programs were distracting us. By God's grace our kids received an education, but it was costing the church too much, so we had to shut the grade school and day care center down.

Rick Warren, author of *The Purpose Driven Life* spoke volumes to me when he said that he had allowed people to persuade him into embracing their ideas or programs, and in doing so he was the one staffing and paying the bills that came along with their ideas. "I let them talk me into something I wasn't excited about," he candidly shared. Sounded all too familiar to me.

After attending the school of hard knocks, the voice of wisdom began to speak to him, impressing the need to discover what he was good at and what he wasn't, or whether the vision God gave him included another man's ideas. Then he learned to say 'no' or delegate authority to others who were more gifted in areas he wasn't. Warren has remained faithful to his calling and conviction and doesn't feel one bit guilty when he has to say no.

I also took a personal inventory of my life and ministry and came to discover what I am good at, and what I am not. I am good at motivating people to live by faith, encouraging them to take risks, to do something they've never done before. I'm a visionary. I already knew I had a lousy time counseling church folks so I staffed gifted people to handle those that needed more than a Sunday morning message of encouragement. I am not a micro-manager, never have been; I am good at delegating.

Thank God for the people He continues to send my way that bring insight when I need it most.

⌣

One day while Richard and I were fervently scouting the city for a building, we drove into an area on the edge of town where we passed a handsome building with red Spanish tiles on the roof. The lease on our warehouse was coming to an end, and we had seven months to relocate.

I was taken aback as I recalled the dream the Lord had given me just before going to Bible School. *In that dream I was preaching to a huge crowd in a building in San Jose, a building with a red-tiled roof just like this one.*

We struck a deal for the 54,000 square-foot building. The monthly payment would be $50,000.00, a high price indeed. But it was time to take another leap of faith. This was literally my dream come true.

> *And believers were increasingly added to the Lord, multitudes of both men and women.* ~ACTS 5:14

CHAPTER 8

TIME OF TESTING

In early 1985 the American computer industry was hit hard when Japan practically took over the semiconductor business. My phone was ringing off the hook with prayer requests from families who were losing their jobs and homes. Many people moved to Oregon or Montana to make a new start.

The church's income leveled off - not a good sign in light of our recent plan to move into the new 2,000 seat sanctuary! My only consolation was remembering how mini-revivals had rallied the people's spirits in the wake of previous relocations.

So, we hosted mini-revival meetings with Rosie Grier who was a former celebrity football player I watched on television for years prior to his conversion. This man was bigger than life yet he was a man who had challenges just like everyone else. "It took me 45 years to realize God had a purpose for bringing me on this earth; for a long time the only thing I was concerned about was running with the football," he preached. "I have purposed in my heart not to fumble the opportunity to carry the Word of God to the world." Through his personal testimony he called the people forward to surrender their lives, their talents and their future to God. We all were stirred and encouraged.

The first celebrity-turned-preacher we hosted at Jubilee was *"Rockin"* Reggie Vinson. At the height of his career he worked with a number of popular artists such as Alice Cooper, John

Lennon, Elvis Presley and Liberace. He went on to become a gospel recording artist, and produced many albums. Reggie and his wife Sadie were genuine, and became lasting friends.

Fall arrived and we were all moved into our new building. We fondly called it *The Bowling Alley* because it didn't look like a typical church building and the ceilings were low. Anticipation and excitement filled the halls of our new building as the staff prepared for our dedication service. Friday, October 18th was a memorable day in the Bernal family archives, not just as a day of celebration but the day that I endured the excruciating pain of a kidney stone.

We had a whole host of guests come out to celebrate with us and Channel 42 was filming the dedication service, live. I gritted my teeth in pain and let the celebration continue. Everyone was excited and I doubt that most knew the pain I was in. Immediately after the service my wife and a few friends rushed me to the hospital emergency room for treatment.

Amidst the uncertainty of the economic boom, I was excited that we were finally leasing a building for the next seven years. We were five-years-old and I remember feeling a sense of permanency. We had never remained anywhere for more than 18 months and now we had a place to call "church."

I was hyped-up with enthusiasm. *Here we are in our new modern building. It won't be long before we fill this place up and have to expand to two services.*

But the surge did not come. In fact, we dropped slightly in attendance. The offerings remained under par. *What is going on here?* I wondered.

Some people said that it was because we had moved out to the *boon docks*, and that we were too far away from the population center of San Jose. Others felt the church had finally arrived, and we didn't need any more growth. What I didn't realize at the time was that the empty field right across the street would be the place for our future sanctuary — a $40 million dollar property that would one day be ours. We would see that dream come to pass 13 years later – in 1997.

But, I'm getting a little ahead of myself, again.

I began a teaching series on *Blood Covenant,* one of my favorite classes in Bible School. I knew it was a critical teaching that I would be sharing with the church because it so liberated my thinking and my approach to God. Most of my teachings for the first 10 years at Jubilee came from understanding that covenant. Blood covenant takes a lot of emotion and guess-work out of God's dealings with man. I have a contract with God through the blood of Jesus and we are bound together, regardless of Satan's plans to thwart my life.

As we turned the corner into 1986, I felt increasingly frustrated.

"Lord, are you through with me here?" I asked. *"Have I taken this church as far as I can? Should I turn it over to another?"* There was no answer.

One Sunday morning from the pulpit, I let my feelings all hang out and shared my perplexity. People thought that I was leaving, so some of them up and left that very week. Friends began calling from around the country asking if I was resigning.

Great, this is just great, Bernal. Your pity party is about to explode in your face. You had better rally the troops quickly and get back on track, I exhorted myself.

It took some time, but I finally convinced the church that I was staying at the helm no matter what.

KOREA'S PRAYER MOUNTAIN

About this time one of our members, Sophia Choi Yu, a precious little Korean lady, told me that a very special person wanted to meet me. Dr. David Yonggi Cho's mother-in-law was in town, and Sophia had told her about me. *"Hallelujah Momma,"* was the name she was affectionately known by.

We made our way to the Prayer Mountain down in Santa Cruz where I met "Momma." Hearing her preach on prayer and fasting, with Sophia interpreting, I knew she would inspire and encourage our church. So I invited her and in her fiery style of preaching she stirred the people and at the end of the service she prayed over them. Her prayer for our church was that we would experience great church growth like the revival in Korea. After the service she invited me to speak at PRAYER MOUNTAIN in Seoul, Korea.

Wow, Dr Cho's famous Prayer Mountain that we've all heard about, I thought excitedly.

In May of 1986, 22 of us left for Seoul, a trip destined to change my life and the focus of my church. Hallelujah Momma had me preaching all over town. My friend and Jubilee's Executive Elder, Dr. Paul Dennis Kim, interpreted for me. Carla and I were having a terrific time exploring the sights of this great nation that was experiencing revival. The Korean *kimchi* was great!

My first visit to Prayer Mountain was an eye-opener. Driving up a winding road to the top, I saw a monumental auditorium built of concrete and wood. The chapel holds 15,000 people.

Run by Pastor Cho's Yoido Full Gospel Church, Prayer Mountain is completely self-sufficient. They grow their own rice and vegetables, and keep chickens and cows.

Prayer Mountain is a site for pilgrimages. The prior year 1.2 million people had visited the mountain, some even fasting and seeking the Lord for weeks at a time. There are hundreds of' prayer grottos scattered throughout the area - small concrete bunkers in which a single person can kneel on a straw mat, close the door and be alone with God.

The compound sits just 8 miles from the Demilitarized Zone that separates North and South Korea. Dr. Cho's congregation view themselves as prayer warriors, and pray daily for the reunification of Korea. They rebuke the powers of darkness in active spiritual warfare. I was impressed by the economic growth of South Korea and the great spiritual vitality of her people.

Dr. Cho's testimony reveals that as a teenager he was converted from Buddhism on his death-bed. He has faithfully followed the Lord's direction all these years in spite of the incredible opposition he faced along the way.

Walking into the church service that weekend, I was in awe at the mass of people coming in and out of the church building. As we were seated we donned head phones attached to our seat and listened to an interpreter translate the entire service.

To watch them take an offering was amazing. When they prayed over the offering you would have thought they were trying to *raise someone from the dead.* The entire congregation was in one accord. Koreans know how to hound heaven in prayer and when they unite together, it truly sounds like a mighty rushing wind. Observing how this church is run like a well-oiled machine, I began thinking about our little church. By comparison, their children's church attendance alone was much more than our entire congregation.

We were ushered past the crowds into Dr. Cho's office for a brief visit. I was a bit nervous meeting him, extending my hand and bowing my head in respect as I greeted him. His demeanor appeared extremely professional, he was a bit stoic and wasn't very cordial. I chalked it up to him being very busy running the world's largest church; I was just honored to have met a real saint of God. As we left his office, bustling through the crowds of people as they made their way out of the church, I was drawn to a long wall situated next to the sanctuary that contained hundreds of what looked like small mailbox slots in a post office. I asked my elder what they were for and he told me that when people join the church they are issued a membership number and a box with a key. This was how they were instructed to pay their weekly tithes. And these boxes were inside the church at numerous locations for easy access. Boy, for a church of their size they have thought of everything.

I struck up a conversation with some of Dr. Cho's leaders regarding his ability to keep this huge church in ship-shape order and still thrive. The Korean church runs on a cell system where they have Sunday celebration services, and during the week they meet in small cell groups. The everyday life of the church occurs in the cell; that is where the people are truly cared for, recognizing it's impossible for the pastor to minister to each member, individually.

As soon as we returned home I re-instituted daily prayer times with fasting, encouraged members to witness, and sought to worship God in our services. The Lord guided me to focus on faith and covenant living, righteousness and other basic doctrinal truths. Getting back to the fundamentals of our Christian faith did wonders for our church. As a result, attendance and offerings began to increase.

Reflecting on my new insight from Korea regarding their cells, my impetuous nature got the best of me and we began a new cell ministry called *Home Fellowship Groups*. I knew we weren't like the Koreans in their discipline of prayer and church attendance, but I thought we would come up with something similar to integrate with our fast-paced Silicon Valley lifestyle. We were experiencing supernatural growth that I wanted to make sure no one slipped through the cracks and believed that this was the solution. In hindsight, I came to realize that it was premature because we didn't have the proper leadership training in place to implement a cell program.

We continued to struggle through the years with different home fellowship programs. It wasn't until we shifted into the Government of 12 cell vision that we found the ultimate solution.

"God is Able"

About this time we made a key change in our approach to worship. Carla and I felt like we had fallen into a predictable routine of singing the same old songs Sunday after Sunday. It seemed to be putting our people to sleep. I wanted to wake everyone up!

A friend told me of a gospel singer named Ron Kenoly who was looking for a position. "He sounds just like *Lou Rawls*," my friend said.

"Lou Rawls," Carla blurted out, "I love Lou Rawls."

We arranged for Ron to come to Jubilee and sing a couple of songs. Ron took the microphone and opened his mouth. It didn't take Carla ten seconds to make up her mind. "Hire him tonight," she said, with a look of assurance.

"Hey, I thought I was the impetuous one," I said in exasperation.

"Okay, sweetheart, if you think so, so be it." Friends, that was one of my better decisions over the last 15 years of ministry. My wife's spiritual intuition proves to be right on the money nine times out of ten. Though I get annoyed about how right she can be, I really respect her guidance when the Lord moves on her.

Ron has become a globally recognized and sought after worship leader. Some call him the *Billy Graham* of praise and worship. His CD's, videos, and cassettes sell by the millions.

Recently someone asked me if I was jealous over Ron's astounding success. "Are you kidding?" I replied. "Ron's success is my success. It's Jubilee's success. We all benefit from what God does through Ron and his gift."

And Ron mobilized a mighty army of skilled musicians and singers that filled Jubilee Christian Center with praise to the Lord Jesus Christ as never before. Not only did some people return to our church, hundreds more started coming for the first time, and joined our family.

I learned a great lesson in 1986. Thank God for new buildings, but in the end these structures are merely brick and mortar. The heartbeat of a growing church is doing the Father's will, welcoming the Holy Spirit, and loving Jesus as He loves us.

And when he had consulted with the people he appointed those who should sing to the Lord, and who should praise the beauty of holiness, as they went out before the army and were saying: Praise the Lord, for His mercy endures forever. ~II CHRONICLES 20:21

∾ DR. CHO'S ADVISORY BOARD

In the spring of 1987, Dr. Cho called me wanting to preach at Jubilee. I was quite surprised, recalling my previous visit with him. I wasn't going to pass up the chance, though.

We were playing golf one morning during his visit and we began talking about ministry and our own personal struggles, when Dr. Cho reminded me about my earlier visit to Korea. He was very apologetic about his demeanor and told me that he had been angry with his mother-in-law and didn't want to associate with any of her *cronies*, ushering us out the door after our very brief visit. I told him I was surprised that he would see us, knowing he was a very busy man. Dr. Cho's warmth and candor were refreshing and inviting to me. He is a man who knows his Source and from whence his success comes and attributes it all to Jesus his Lord.

We were at the second hole on the green when he asked me if I would like to come and preach at his Church Growth International (CGI) Conference in Seoul later that year. In the next breath he asked me if I would consider being on his Advisory Board. I was honored and thrilled, yet speechless – Gulp! – *I must keep my composure in front of this spiritual giant in the faith*, I thought. I was calm on the outside, but inside I was doing somersaults. I played horrible golf that day, I'm sure. My mind was blown away at his graciousness toward me, a man so highly regarded. Who was I?

Carla and I have since made annual pilgrimages to Seoul to study the revival there and to be inspired and strengthened in our faith as we broaden our vision for more than what we have today. With the size of Dr. Cho's church, who can argue with that kind of success?

"God is already giving me favor with people in high places," I'm beginning to realize. Why me? Is it just another coincidence? Continue reading.

✎ TRAVELOGUE DESTINATION: *BEIJING*

Chinese evangelist, the late Nora Lam, and her family joined our church, and before long Carla and I had become good friends with them. Nora was always after me to go with her to China. One afternoon at church, the late Dottie Bankus, our resident prophetess, came up to me and said, "Pastor, the Lord wants you to go to China soon."

I told the Lord I was not going unless He provided tickets for Carla, the children, and me. Plus, I needed to feel a witness in my spirit about going. The very next Sunday a family told us they would pick up the tab for Carla and me, Jesse and Sarah, and would provide us with spending money to boot.

On December 27, 1987, we left San Francisco for Taiwan and mainland China. Our dear friends, Dr. James Pippin and his wife, Alene, were traveling with Nora. We also met Paul and Jan Crouch of *Trinity Broadcasting Network,* who were very friendly. As soon as our group entered communist China, we could all sense the demonic spirit of oppression. I could not help but compare the spiritual exuberance of South Korea to the fearful restriction of Red China. Perhaps someday a great Pentecostal wave will wash over the Chinese mainland. Why not?

Eventually we reached Beijing. The oppressive atmosphere intensified in the capitol city that controls all of Red China. That morning, we received an audience with the Assistant Ambassador from the United States to China. He told us of the great changes in China since President Nixon's visit in the early 1970s. As a result, the Bamboo Curtain had come down, and the Chinese were open to exchanges with the Western world; they had a desperate need for technology and innovative ideas.

The underground church in China is alive and flourishing, but it is in dire need of tools for evangelism. Nora introduced me to a Chinese pastor who spent 22 years in prison because of his faith. Two of his fingers had been cut off in an attempt to break his spirit. I will never forget that man's eyes, how peaceful and kind they were.

Bernal, are you made out of the stuff this man is? I asked myself silently, looking at all the fingers and two thumbs on my hands.

"I'm glad my children are here to see all this, Lord," I whispered. "Thank you."

As we left the little church, Paul Crouch slipped the pastor a love offering and patted him on the back. I, too, followed suit. As I handed him an envelope, I looked into the Chinese pastor's eyes again.

Oh, God, keep me sweet and humble, please, I prayed as we

walked down the back stairs into the cool, Chinese night.

During our stay in Beijing, I periodically awakened from a deep sleep, sensing a presence in the room - an evil sinister personality. One night I bolted up in bed and saw a shadowy apparition dart away. I woke up Carla and we began to pray out loud for the blood of Jesus to cover the room and the demons to depart.

The next day, we visited China's *Great Wall*, a real monument of human endeavor. Matt Crouch, Paul and Jan's youngest son had brought television equipment to capture the trip and show it back home on the network. As Paul, Nora, and Jan were being taped, sharing about their dreams and desires for China, they broke into intercessory prayer. Jan had a vision of a ruling prince swooping down at them. It was a hideous, evil-looking spirit, unhappy with our intrusion on its turf. Jan began shouting the name of Jesus and pointing her finger at the principality, and he vanished.

That day at lunch, Paul and I discussed how spiritual warfare involves pulling down strongholds over cities, even whole nations. We stated our agreement with Pastor Jack Hayford that cities, whether American or Chinese, need to be taken back from the enemy by the prayers of anointed Christians.

The previous month, I had been at *Church on the Way* in Van Nuys, California, at a ministers' conference hosted by Pastor Jack Hayford. The theme of the conference was *Taking Your Cities for God*. Every speaker shared that it was essential for the principality over a city to be disarmed first in order for revival to break out. My heart was stirred as never before.

After lunch on the way back to our hotel, I made up my mind to spend 1988 researching my city, San Jose, and even the nation, to see if the ruling principalities could be located, identified, and evicted. Dr. Pippin encouraged me to put my research into a book, which I did in the latter part of 1988. The book was entitled, *Storming Hell's Brazen Gates.*

I didn't realize it then but on our China mission we were foreshadowing a bold venture into the heart of Communist darkness after the Tiananmen Square massacre that would take place two years later.

Back in the States, Paul invited Carla and me to host the TBN *"Praise the Lord"* program a number of times. We often ministered on the subject of spiritual warfare.

⌣

One spring afternoon in 1988 my trusted friend and confidante, Richard Cardoza came to my office to tell me of a dream he had and how this dream confirmed that it was time for him and his family to once again move. He believed it was time to pastor his own church. We had both known this to be the will of the Lord for some time. Nonetheless it would seem strange for Richard and Corrine not to be with us, because they have always been more than friends; we consider them a part of our extended family.

Today Richard and Corrine are pastoring a growing church in the Sacramento, California area – *The Lord's Church* - and we feel proud to be a part of it.

WOLF IN SHEEP'S CLOTHING

For the sake of anonymity, I'll call the man I refer to as Darren. At a time when I was looking for an assistant, Darren appeared and had been a member of Jubilee since 1985. His credentials were impeccable. He had worked for a national ministry, and had been ordained with a major Pentecostal denomination. But just as Lucifer poses as an angel of light, so too are those in the church who harbor dark intentions.

As the Cardoza's were transitioning, Darren moved right in to become my associate so I was able to watch him up close. He had been teaching and ministering in the church and everyone seemed to take a liking to him. To all appearances, he was an effective leader who inspired those around him and worked tirelessly. What I didn't know was that the man was a pedophile. He began preying on young men in our church.

A mother who was a member of our church was working on a hunch that her son, who had struggled with homosexuality before attending Jubilee, was involved with Darren.

I summoned Darren to my office to respond to the accusation before he heard it from anyone else. Darren exploded into rage and vigorously denied the charges. He pounded on my desk, proclaiming his righteous life. Darren's defense sounded so plausible that I hoped he was telling the truth.

That very day Carla and I talked with the young man's parents. They agreed to allow me to talk to the young man alone. He confirmed my worst fear about Darren.

A familiar feeling from childhood wrapped its scaly arms around me. I felt ashamed. Why hadn't I seen through the sheepskin into Darren's wolfish heart? *This will be the end of Jubilee,* I'm sure.

We confronted Darren with the facts. He resigned immediately.

The following Wednesday night Carla, Pastor Brian (who had now become my new music pastor since Ron Kenoly was now traveling extensively and unable to keep up with pastoring the music department) and I, went to visit Darren at his home. I felt worse than being at a funeral. Darren admitted to some of the charges, telling us he felt he was in a pit with a monster. He rationalized that if he didn't involve himself in certain activities, the monster would devour him. Carla broke down and wept.

We immediately reported the allegations to the *Child Protective Services,* because it was the right and lawful thing to do. The future of Jubilee was at stake.

The police arrested Darren. But when interrogated, he sang a different tune. No longer repentant, he vehemently denied the charges. According to him, everyone was lying, including me. The story hit the news and traveled far and fast. Even Pastor Cho in South Korea read about it in a local Seoul newspaper. He called to offer me hope and support.

I broke the news to the church, doing my best to sound merciful, yet strong. But I wanted to bury my head in the sand.

Later, after being in and out of jail and attending criminal proceedings Darren was finally sentenced to 19 years in prison.

❧ OUR SAFEGUARDS

Unfortunately, we lost a number of Jubilee families because of this. What hurt the most was that people whom I had married, visited in the hospital, and vacationed with, bolted from the church. The wound was deeper than anyone will ever know.

To help me through the ordeal, my former secretary, Virginia, faithfully shielded me from angry and acidic letters that poured into my office. Staffers, George Richardson and

Mark Miller, were my saving grace too. Their experience had much to do with helping me through this ordeal.

This experience was a rude awakening for us. It taught us the potential vulnerability and ignorance that church leaders fall prey to when someone slithers through their front door to do harm, under the cover of good intentions. We want to believe that everyone who comes to church has the right motives.

Our church now has state-of-the-art security systems in place and safeguards in our hiring practices, including finger-printing and background checks to ensure nothing like this occurs again. In addition, I have counseled some twenty to thirty pastors all over America who have faced similar situations who believe that they can never recover from this kind of devastating experience – but the truth is – they can. It may take two or three years for the dust to settle, but a church can indeed get past this type of a nightmare.

> *Beware of false prophets, who come to you in sheep's clothing, but inwardly they are ravenous wolves.* ~MATTHEW 7:15

I can attest to the highs and lows in establishing the kingdom of God. But for every down there are abundantly more highs!

Resurrection weekend at the Flint Center on the De Anza College Campus in Cupertino was a highlight that year with Ron Kenoly's *"He's Alive"* musical cantata. It was a dramatic portrayal of the life and ministry of Jesus Christ, culminating with a glorious celebration of the Resurrection. Every year it was a treat to see Ron's musicals. Ron is more than just a world-renowned worship leader; he is quite a talented arranger, producer and songwriter. To think that he labored with us for all those years before God released him to his next assignment. We were truly blessed.

〰 OUR JERUSALEM - *ALVISO*

We were beginning to focus on our newest Jerusalem – Alviso. It was inevitable that we would focus on this little village town, as it is a stone's throw away from us situated at the head of the San Francisco Bay. Once a seaport and center for weekend boat builders and yachtsmen, it's now a marina completely silted in. Over 5,000 people lived in this run down, forgotten corner of San Jose. Mostly of Mexican-American decent, many of the people were poor, illiterate and most of all living far below God's best. We adopted them and began providing humanitarian relief to help take care of them. It is obvious in Scripture that God has a very tender spot in His heart for the poor.

Psalm 82:3-4 declares, *"Defend the poor and fatherless; do justice to the afflicted and needy...free them from the hand of the wicked."*

During a routine visit in the neighborhood one sunny afternoon some concerned residents of the community informed us that the City of San Jose was targeting a group of residents near the swamps to evict them from their shanty dwellings. "They have nowhere to go," cried one of the residents.

Alviso had many problems, not the least of which was the gradual sinking of the shoreline due to the reduction of the water table. This required higher levees to keep the San

Francisco Bay from engulfing the town as it did during the flood of 1983.

Indeed, the City needed to evacuate these residents for safety reasons, but it was the way they wanted to go about doing it. Being forearmed we went to bat for these defenseless people. When the City realized that Jubilee Christian Center was getting involved they backed off and willingly agreed to help relocate them.

Today the landscape of this little village town is changing. The value of real estate is soaring, with a fairly new golf range and club, and hundred-thousand-dollar townhouses that line the tail end of First Street. *Val's Restaurant* has changed little since 1941. It's so close to the church campus, I come by for lunch every now and again, and they're still serving some of my favorite home-cooked meals. The homey atmosphere reminds me of the good ole' days; service is still provided by most of the original waitresses. *"If your grandmother didn't make it... Val's doesn't serve it."* I found out recently that Mom and Emmett would occasionally frequent the restaurant for dinner, too.

LOMA PRIETA EARTHQUAKE

Friday, October 11, 1989 - the Oakland A's were playing the San Francisco Giants in the World Series at Candlestick Park. Millions of television viewers watching the game were eyewitnesses of the 6.9 magnitude Loma Prieta earthquake shortly after the game started as it walloped Northern California with a bucking shaker at 5:04 pm.

As the hours unfolded, the quake transformed a handful of folks at the flash points of damage into a live cast of victims and survivors. Fear hit thousands in the Bay Area as they tried to make their way home amidst the gridlock of traffic that swelled the freeways and streets. The quake disrupted the electrical grid and power outages were everywhere. People were running aimlessly through the streets, not knowing what to do. The panic-stricken drove into gas stations only to find long lines at the gas pump. Others made their way to grocery stores to stock up on emergency supplies. Convenience stores were closing their doors to prevent looting and to clean up the food and other merchandise that was strewn all over the floor.

Our church house was filled to overflowing with people looking for emotional support. In times like these, pastors become the only support many have, and we were doing our best to help especially those directly affected by the quake.

Dr. Cho was in town to speak at the evening service and I was on my way back to the office when the quake occurred. As I drove into the parking lot I could feel the earth moving and wondered what was going on. As I sat in my car watching the asphalt rolling up and down in a rippling motion, I began to realize we were having a major earthquake and my instincts kicked in, *"Where are my kids? I need to get them to safety."* I ran into the office and found out that they were safely under a table with one of their teachers.

For months after the earthquake we watched the aftermath of the devastation on television. The buckling of the Cypress Freeway and the lives sandwiched between its metal and concrete was nightmarish. The Santa Cruz mountains to the south of us were hard hit and one area was split like a whacked watermelon.

My son called me much later that evening and told me that

he had been at the World Series on the upper deck watching the game, "I was shocked and in fear and didn't know what was going to happen; players and fans alike bolted to the open field, under doorways and anywhere else they thought it would be safe; it was sheer pandemonium, Dad."

"The game was cancelled, but it took another four nail-biting hours to drive back home on the quake-battered roads," Adam recounted his day. As he continued telling me the details I could tell he was shaken to the core – it was an awakening of sorts.

ADAM JOINS OUR RANKS

It was late at night and two weeks after the earthquake when Adam dropped by to visit his dad.

"Honey, wake up, it's Adam, he wants to talk to you," my anxious wife shook me awake. As I got out of bed and put my robe on I went to the living room to see what Adam wanted. This was not to be a casual time of catching up. His eyes were red and puffy. I motioned him to follow me into my office and there we sat and talked for hours.

"You okay, son?" I asked.

"Dad, I've got to get right with God," my number one son exclaimed. I had led Adam to Christ when he was 12-years-old while we were fishing out at my favorite bass lake. In fact, Adam was my first convert.

But like many new converts, Adam faced numerous pressures from society and his peers that eventually undermined his faith. Carla and I agreed we wouldn't pressure him to attend church with us. We simply prayed for him, knowing that one day he would make the right choice.

Now, at 25 years of age, the Holy Spirit was moving on Adam in a most intriguing way. He and his girlfriend were headed up to Lake Tahoe to party. But during the drive, his girlfriend began reading him one of my books. She read the part about how after a long life of self-will I had finally surrendered everything to Jesus. The words "surrender everything" kept going through his mind, coupled with the fact that he was still shaken by the earthquake at Candlestick Park two weeks prior.

Conviction fell on Adam. He turned the car around and headed home. In my home office that night Adam and I prayed together and he rededicated his life to Christ. Wow! There is no feeling like helping your own child find God!

From the first week he was saved he began traveling with me everywhere. Within the first year of his salvation he met and broke bread with Dr. Cho, Oral Roberts, Dr. Kenneth Hagin, Dr. Lester Sumrall, and so many other high profile Christian leaders. He had no clue who these people were and what impact they were having on Christendom. Christians who know these people at a distance would give anything to be in an intimate gathering with them. Sounds like my early years in ministry. I also talked Adam into enrolling in our Bible College a year later.

Before becoming a senior pastor, Adam was also our youth pastor, and activities director at our San Jose campus. The day I hired Adam to work for me Carla said to me, "Hey Pastor Dad, how's it feel to have both your red-headed sons under one roof?"

Today, Adam is Pastor Adam Bernal, senior pastor of *Jubilee Tri-Valley* in Livermore, CA. I married my son and his wife Michelle on September 20, 1997. They have a daughter, Hannah who is now four years old.

One day I had a commitment to give the devotional prayer at a Sunday lunch with *First Lady* Barbara Bush. "I want you to take over the third Sunday morning service," I told Adam.

"What'll I say, Dad?" he asked, looking a little nervous. "Just relax and talk from your heart," I coached, "God will do the rest."

I was one proud father when my son took the pulpit to preach his first sermon. God is good, isn't He!

> *As for me and my house, we will serve the Lord.*
> ~JOSHUA 24:15

TIANANMEN SQUARE

As my spiritual history unfolded, I found myself returning to China in early 1990.

The air was icy cold in January when a small army of God's prayer warriors, clutching official papers, marched into the middle of Tiananmen Square. Suspicious government soldiers eyed us every step of the way. What had brought us there?

On June 3rd and 4th, 1989, the People's Liberation Army had brutally crushed pro-democracy supporters in Tiananmen Square, killing an estimated 3,000-5,000 people, injuring another 10,000, and arresting hundreds of students and workers. The violent suppression of the Tiananmen Square protest caused widespread international condemnation of the Chinese government.

Political strings had to be pulled before our small group was allowed out onto the square. Soldiers marching in cadence kept peering at us.

The square itself is enormous. It seemed to take forever to make our way to the center. I looked down at the tank tracks and bullet holes carved into the pavement - a silent memorial to the thousands who died for freedom.

Ron Kenoly led us in praise and worship. Rachel Flores, one of my personal intercessors, got a little loud. I wondered if we weren't going to get thrown off the premises. Rachel fueled Carla and Nora, and before long we were having a real deliverance service. Soon our quiet little prayer group had strapped on their armor and we were battling in the spirit for the world's largest nation.

I opened a bottle of anointing oil and poured it onto the square as a prophetic act for the remission of sins against the Chinese people by their communist leaders.

After about 30 minutes we slowly made our way back to our vehicles. I couldn't help but catch a look at a few of the soldiers on our way out. I leaned over to Carla and Nora and said, "Now they know we're all nuts." We nervously chuckled and headed for our hotel.

That first Sunday I had the privilege of preaching in one of China's largest Christian churches. This was not an underground house church, but a government sanctioned movement. Pastor Kan, the senior minister, was genuinely friendly and cordial. He really seemed excited that Ron was going to sing "Amazing Grace" for his congregation. This pastor told Nora that I could have 30 minutes to preach on anything I wanted.

Ron sang like only Ron can sing. Then I took the pulpit with my interpreter. I was told that Billy Graham was the only other

Christian from the states allowed to have this liberty. *Boy, tough act to follow,* I told myself.

As I looked over the crowd I spotted several men from the Secret Police, obviously monitoring my message. Instead of teaching, I simply shared my testimony of how I came to Christ. The people laughed and clapped. Many wept.

I prayed that China's people would continue to grow in Christ, and would learn to call upon the Holy Spirit for the power to carry out spiritual warfare.

> *All authority has been given to Me in heaven and on earth. Go therefore and make disciples of all the nations, baptizing them in the name of the Father and of the Son and of the Holy Spirit, teaching them to observe all things that I have commanded you; and lo, I am with you always, even to the end of the age.* ~MATTHEW 28:18-20

THE ARGENTINE REVIVAL

Television afforded me the privilege of being invited to cities all over America and abroad to preach, especially on the subject of spiritual warfare. My bags remained packed, always hopping on a plane traveling somewhere or another. I didn't mind, though, because when you are called, God equips you and you learn to go with the flow.

"Dick, I want you to come with me to Argentina in October" my dear friend Dr. Ed Silvoso pled in his thick South American accent.

He continued, "I want you to witness firsthand the revival

fires of this land. I am gathering the national leaders who were instrumental in the genesis of the revival that is sweeping Argentina."

Ed's ministry, *Harvest Evangelism* is headquartered here in San Jose and he had been inviting me to go with him to Argentina for some time. He knew that I was a student of spiritual warfare, revival and church growth, and was sure I would benefit greatly from this trip.

This being my first visit to the South American continent, I was curious and excited for the opportunity. It was my second chance to see a nation in revival – Korea being my first.

Comprising almost the entire southern half of South America, Argentina is the world's 8th largest county. We flew into the capital city of Buenos Aries for a brief visit, taking in a city tour and sights unique to this bustling metropolis. The lifestyle and architecture have a European flare of sophistication that is remarkably distinctive. We savored a plate of their famous Argentine cattle beef; was it delicious! The next morning we flew to our destination city, *Resistencia*, situated in northeast Argentina.

The church services were filled with exuberant worship as massive groups of people gathered together day and night to pray for and evangelize the city. People from all walks of life attended and the altar calls were almost beyond belief. The crowds were electrified. I was seeing things I had never seen before. I had the opportunity to view major deliverances right before my eyes. It was nothing short of phenomenal.

During the day a group of us were escorted throughout the various neighborhoods, businesses and churches in the city to see firsthand just how powerful spiritual warfare had affected this city, turning many of those gathering places into sanctuaries for the presence of the Lord. One of the pastors was having 5 to 6 church services a day, seven-days-a-week. I had been preaching about the dynamics of spiritual warfare everywhere I went, and to see, once again, the fruit of this type of prayer was undeniable. This encouraged me greatly to know that we were on the right track.

Thanks to Dr. Ed Silvoso, another highlight of this trip was the quality time I was able to spend with the spiritual gatekeepers of the city, including powerful men such as Carlos Annacondia, Omar Cabrera, Norberto Carlini and Hector Jimenez. Dining with them each evening, absorbing their captivating accounts of miracles God had been doing over the years was boosting my faith. After all, these men were becoming veterans of revival. Talking until the wee hours of the morning, I too wanted answers to some of the dilemmas and obstacles we faced in having revival in our city. This was yet another missionary excursion that was igniting the fires of revival in me.

Little did I know that 10 years later I would have another opportunity to see another South American city in the throes of revival – Bogotá, Columbia!

Part Three

Warfare And The Kingdom

For we do not wrestle against flesh and blood,

but against principalities, against powers,

against the rulers of the darkness of this age,

against spiritual hosts of wickedness

in the heavenly places.

-Ephesians 6:12

CHAPTER 9

TAKING YOUR CITY FOR GOD

After writing my first book *Storming Hell's Brazen Gates,* I became known for my teaching on spiritual warfare. The catalyst for the personal revelation I received in this book came to me when Dr. Lester Sumrall was in town visiting several years prior. We went golfing and I asked him to help me understand Dr. David Yonggi Cho's work in Korea, a man with a church of 800,000 members in a pagan land. I understood the practical mechanics of running a church of that magnitude through the cell system but, spiritually, how did he accomplish this?

His answer was so simple and profound that it floored me:

> *"They bound the strong man; they pulled down*
> *the prince from his perch. Heaven opened; revival*
> *fell."*

I later heard Dr. Cho's insights on the matter in greater detail and wish to share them with you.

> My ministry started with city-taking. When I
> first pioneered my church, nobody would come to
> our old, torn Marine surplus tent because there
> was great demonic oppression over the village.
> The key to breaking that bondage was the casting

out of a demon from a woman who had lain paralyzed for seven years. When, after months of prayer, the demon oppressing her was cast out and she was healed, our church exploded with growth. The sky above the village was broken open and the blessings of God began pouring down...

The growth of our church and the growth of Christianity throughout the nation of Korea did not come by accident. It came through fervent, violent, prevailing prayer. As Jesus said in Matthew 11:12, *"The kingdom of heaven suffers violence, and the violent take it by force."*

For example, in our church we have all-night prayer meetings where thousands come to pray. On Friday evenings, more than 15,000 people join hearts and hands to pray for the coming of the kingdom of God. On Prayer Mountain, at least 3,000 people are praying, fasting, and ministering unto the Lord on any given day. In all, one-and-a-half million people visit and pray there in any given year.

This is not limited only to our church; all over South Korea Christians are praying. One of the most unique characteristics of the Korean church is that millions gather early every morning at 5:30 to pray despite wind, rain, or snow.

The kingdom of God indeed suffered violence in Korea. There was a long history of persecuting Christians by the Communists as well as by the Japanese occupation forces. For instance, the Japanese installed Shinto altars in all Christian churches. The military police stood guard to enforce the law that required all Christians to bow down to the Shinto altar before entering to worship Almighty God. Those who refused were jailed and punished severely, and many ministers were executed at the hands of the Japanese forces.

Many churches corporately decided to oppose this injustice. Those churches were locked, with women and children inside, and burned to the ground due to their refusal to worship idols. Until recently, it took great sacrifice to be a Christian in Korea. Believers were a minority. But now, because the "blood of the martyrs is the seed of the church," we count at least one-fourth of our nation to be believers in the Lord Jesus Christ.

Open portal Above Pensacola

I arrived into my office for a brief visit before we closed for Christmas one busy afternoon. My sister Judy, who was our receptionist at the time said "A Pastor John Kilpatrick from Florida wants to talk to you today. He said it was urgent."

His name didn't seem to ring a bell with me but I felt I should return his call. When I reached him on the phone he said, "Maybe you've heard of my church..." As he mentioned the location and the details, I remembered hearing of a revival breaking out in an Assembly of God church in Florida. I had read about it in a Charisma magazine. The sleepy coastal town of Pensacola, home of the Navy Blue Angels, was inundated with hungry people seeking a fresh touch from God. Church attendees would line up in front of the church beginning in the wee hours of the morning just to find a seat for the evening service. It was not uncommon to see people from all walks of life responding to altar calls every night for years. The continual miraculous daily outpouring of the glory of God put Pensacola on the map and spawned other similar revivals in Missouri, Iowa, Michigan, and elsewhere. At the time there were reportedly 1.4 million visitors; 85,000 converts with church services five nights a week.

Later Evangelist Steve Hill came preaching blistering calls to repentance and holiness, and finally the outpouring gushed out and extended world-wide. Most of my staff including Carla and my kids attended the revival; my daughter Sarah was impacted greatly for months afterward, saying it was a turning point in her young life. Soon after, 200-300 of my church members shuttled back and forth to Pensacola to experience first-hand Brownsville's glorious encounters with God.

To my utter amazement Kilpatrick proceeded to explain, "Pastor Dick you have no idea the role you played in this revival. The book you put together, *Storming Hell's Brazen Gates,* revolutionized my thinking. Back in 1990 I got a copy of it and I taught my church from the book and we did what the book said to do; heaven opened and we've been in revival since. I've been asked to write a book about this revival and to do that I must quote your book. I need your permission to do so."

I responded to him, "Quote the whole book if you want to, but what I don't get is - I write the book and you get the revival!"

Pastor Kilpatrick remarked, "But it is working for you in a different place, India."

"God sure works in mysterious ways," I thought as I hung up the phone that day.

It is amazing to me that this uncomplicated pioneering book, *STORMING*, was used in such a unique way. It was the watershed publication of my Christian life. Because Carla and I were regular hosts of the TBN *"Praise the Lord"* program during that time, my book was introduced and promoted on the air and reached nearly 80 countries. The inquiries regarding this book came in bucketfuls each day. It was soon written in several languages, and spread all over India. It went out of print, but later I republished it.

If we count ourselves as Christ's disciples, we must press forward aggressively to take a stand against the *god of this age* who continually blinds the minds of unbelievers and prevents them from seeing the truth of the gospel.

With all the experience and insight I was gaining in my travels abroad and here at home, I wrote another book similar to my first and it's become very popular – *Curses, What They are and How To Break Them*. It never ceases to amaze me everywhere I go, the insatiable interest and hunger people have on these subject matters. People's eyes are opening and their hearts are being drawn towards God to rid themselves, their families, and their communities of the demonic interference that is often deeply entrenched.

The divine networking that was going on in my life was a constant flow that allowed me to continue meeting dignitaries, high profile Christians, and the like.

In 1991, through the connection of a pastor friend Harold Caballeros, who was on Dr. Cho's Church Growth International Board, I conducted a Bible Study for the President of Guatemala, *Jorge Antonio Serrano Elas.* Afterwards, he was eager to receive prayer from us. Being the President of a nation presents challenges not known to the average person. To open himself up to others was difficult enough, but in a contrite manner he too recognized he needed divine intervention in the affairs of his life.

Typical of our hosts in the countries we visit, we were given a tour of this cosmopolitan city. Situated on a plateau surrounded by lush green hills and volcanoes of the Sierra Madre, Guatemala City is a city rich with culture and history dating back to the Maya Indians. We couldn't help but notice the vibrant colorful native dress the Guatemalans wore in their open markets. We visited the National Palace, whose interiors are decorated with painted murals that tell the story of Guatemala's history and the *Catedral Metropolitana,* one of the few colonial structures left in the city today. The archeological monuments, natural history and dramatic landscapes added to my memorable travelogue.

Touring a city has a two-fold purpose for me. I not only enjoy history, but my curiosity and interest in the spiritual aspects of a city are instructional. Coming together with the gatekeepers of the city, recognizing that they are the spiritual authority representing God in that city, we gain new insights and strategies for city taking. Our fellowship was rich and instructive as we sampled a traditional Guatemalan dish, *pepian de pollo*. Delicioso!

Every June, we made our annual pilgrimage to Tulsa, Oklahoma to attend the International Charismatic Bible Ministries Conference. I was now a trustee on the organization's board of directors. The teachings and ministry greatly enriched Carla and me. It was also good for us to hear from the leaders of this movement the pulse beat of what they too were experiencing in the world.

SPIRITUAL WARFARE NETWORK

I was introduced to an interesting group of people from the *Spiritual Warfare Network,* (SWN) spearheaded by Dr. C. Peter Wagner, a former professor at Fuller Theological Seminary in Pasadena, California. At the time I was cross-pollinating with leaders in the body of Christ because I knew they could add to God's will in my life and ministry. I was eager to meet the professor. I teased Dr. Wagner that he looked like Kentucky Fried Chicken's *Colonel Sanders.*

My gifting is to teach more by inspiration whereas Dr. Wagner teaches more from the academic viewpoint.

I began to realize that education was necessary but only when it was coupled with inspiration. Things occur in the supernatural that cannot always be explained and academicians like Peter can break it down to give greater understanding to things that are perhaps extra-biblical, but not anti-biblical. If something strange and supernatural occurs, should we discount it altogether or can we allow God to express His sovereignty

155

even though we don't have a chapter and verse to stand on? Peter really helped me to understand parameters doctrinally. It is critical for the body of Christ, especially in the Charismatic movement, to have the *Jack Deere's,* the *Peter Wagner's* and the *Jack Hayford's,* intellectuals to be sure, but who nevertheless love God as much as anyone.

Shortly after meeting the SWN I was in Louisville, Kentucky, invited by a group of leaders hosting a warfare conference in their area. They wanted me to instruct them on territorial spirits, aware that the subject was still very controversial in the Body of Christ, and they needed answers. They were hungry to understand and apply the precepts of spiritual warfare to their city; it was obvious to them that the heavens over them were closed and they desperately wanted breakthrough. An African-American Baptist preacher introduced himself to me after the service one evening and said that he was warned by his leaders not to attend, but he came out of curiosity anyway, "testing the waters."

He continued, "I was checking you and Ron Kenoly out and was drawn to everything you were saying; I enjoyed Ron's music too."

He was a typical inner city African-American Baptist preacher who was hungry for truth.

"Will you come and preach for me next year?" he asked.

I told him I would be delighted to, and as I turned to leave he uttered, "Bring Ron with you, too."

HALLOWEEN NIGHT PRAYER RALLY

I was armed with new understanding and boldness to now

do what no man had done before. Carla and I, together with a well known evangelist from Texas, began praying about gathering 10,000 prayer warriors in downtown San Francisco for a massive prayer rally on Halloween night.

The cosmopolitan city of San Francisco is often compared to Sodom and Gomorrah, cities that were judged for their wickedness. But I prefer to compare it to *Ephesus*, which when warned of judgment repented and came under the grace of God.

The more I considered the idea the more it led to phone calls and divine appointments to bring this idea to fruition. I wanted to offer this as a spiritual alternative to one of the raunchiest Halloween parties in America. Between 300,000 and 500,000 homosexuals, lesbians, witches and *looky-loos* gather in the *Castro District* to party and let it all hang out. Mardi Gras is tame by comparison.

People from Bay Area local churches responded enthusiastically. In fact, we raised nearly $100,000.00 for the event after our normal tithes and offerings.

The press picked up on the event with headlines streaming across the newspapers, *"God's Green Berets invade San Francisco!"* They made us look like right-winged political activists coming to curse gays, liberals, and the city itself. Nothing was further from the truth. Our intention was to offer an alternative on Halloween night by inviting God's love and power into the city of San Francisco.

It was inevitable that two kingdoms would collide.

We soon ran into Dr. Eric J. Pryor, a Wiccan priest of the *Temple of the New Earth*. He was outraged at our plans after reading the articles in the local papers.

To protest the prayer meeting, Eric Pryor busied himself

organizing various pagan and homosexual groups like *Act Up* and *Queer Nation*.

On the morning of my 46th birthday in 1991, I made the front page of the Wall Street Journal. Later I appeared in USA Today and Newsweek. I began furiously fending off calls, reporters, and cameras because everyone wanted more of the story.

CBS TELEVISION TALK SHOW

A local CBS affiliate invited me to a morning talk show called, "People are Talking." They wanted me to explain our purpose for going to San Francisco. To my surprise, I was to be pitted against none other than Dr. Eric Pryor. As Carla and I were ushered into the green room for coffee and make-up, Dr. Pryor joined in for the same.

Eric was a very thin young man with a shock of bleached blond hair, and he wore a priest's collar with a pentagram hanging around his neck.

"Hello, Eric, how are you today?" I asked, sticking out my hand.

Eric looked up sheepishly and put his hand in mine.

"Eric," I said, "after the show how about you and me having lunch? I'd like to explain to you our real purpose for this meeting."

"Sure, I'd be glad to," he replied.

The show host kept trying to pit Eric and me against each other. I didn't take the bait. After the show, Carla and I shared that our reason for the Christian get-together on Halloween was to pray in a positive way for San Francisco. Before long we were witnessing to Eric and his live-in girlfriend Sondra about Jesus. I could see a visible change in his countenance as we talked.

I took a liking to this young couple, and we all laughed together several times during our personal encounter.

On an impulse that I now believe came from the Holy Spirit, I asked Eric to be my special guest at our meeting that evening "Sure, Pastor Dick, I'll go," he responded.

We met him at 6:00 o'clock that evening and made our way to the Civic Auditorium.

We pushed our way through the crowd and into the auditorium. Hundreds from our church shouted and waved to Pastor Dick and Carla, but looked stunned when they saw Eric at our side.

I counted almost 30 news reporters. Most were inching their way toward Eric and me. Eric seemed moved by the message being preached, indeed we all were.

The crowd outside the prayer rally finally dispersed when the police threw a tear gas bomb at them. That's one Halloween I'll never forget!

The day after Halloween, Carla and I gave Eric a Bible and challenged him to dig into the Scriptures and find out for himself who Jesus really is. Eric agreed and we all prayed.

Carla and I stayed in touch with Eric for the next three weeks. We gave him a standing invitation to visit Jubilee for a Sunday service. One morning he came, and at the end of my message, he gave his heart to Christ.

Eric and Sondra were our guests for dinner that Thanksgiving. I looked across the table at this born again soul, as Eric bowed his head in prayer for the meal.

The Spirit of the Lord...has anointed me to preach the gospel to the poor; He has sent me to heal the brokenhearted, to proclaim liberty to the captives...to set at liberty those who are oppressed; to proclaim the acceptable year of the Lord. ~LUKE 4:18-19

SOUTH CENTRAL L.A.

America was stunned by what took place in Los Angeles late in the afternoon of April 29, 1992. South central Los Angeles erupted in rioting, looting, arson, and killing. The immediate cause of the outburst was a jury verdict rendered earlier that day. Four white policemen were found not guilty of assault in the beating of an African-American named Rodney King.

When the violence broke, Los Angeles Mayor Tom Bradley imposed a curfew. Even so, the rioting and looting lasted three days. It was the worst urban disturbance in 20th century America. More than 54 people were killed. Over 5,000 buildings were destroyed or badly damaged. At least 4,000 people were injured and more than 12,000 arrested. Thousands of jobs had been lost and whole neighborhoods wiped out. The rioting got a head start on the police because the verdict was so unexpected, and the reaction so sudden.

Jubilee Christian Center is full of African-Americans, Hispanics, and Koreans. Many had family members and friends in this part of Los Angeles. True to God's call on my life through the symbolic death of my Uncle Dick, I felt we had to do something as a church family. So, the Sunday following the catastrophe, I preached on the *Good Samaritan*. The church responded and I took $50,000.00 out of our general fund, leaving us with a balance of $4,000.00.

I headed south in the company of my wife, Pastor Brian Waller, who is African-American, and Dr. Kim, who is Korean. We were on a mission to bring love and assistance to a hurting city. I felt that the Church ought to be the first involved. We gave the money to a general recovery fund.

Later that day we went to the very spot where the riots broke out. Brian led us in worship. Then we asked God to forgive the sins of the perpetrators of the crimes and to restore the victims who suffered loss and personal tragedy.

We asked the Father for a fresh outpouring of love and spiritual unity to replace the hate and hostility. We finished our prayer time and headed for the airport to return to San Jose. We knew we had done what we could.

> *When they pray toward this place and confess Your name, and turn from their sin...then hear in heaven, and forgive the sin of Your servants...that You may teach them the good way in which they should walk.* ~1 KINGS 8:35-36

HALLOWEEN REUNION AT THE STICK

On Halloween night in 1992, we gathered 20,000 Christians from throughout the Bay Area at the Candlestick Park. The stadium was home to both the San Francisco 49ers and Giants, but with God's help it became a wonderful place for a spiritual event. Eric Pryor sat on the platform with Carla and me, and we once again proclaimed that Jesus is Lord over the whole Bay Area, praying with authority and declaring that the church would recapture this day that Satan has traditionally claimed for his own. We knew Satan wasn't happy with our spiritual efforts, but we pressed on.

When Diane Sawyer of *Prime Time Live* got wind of this, she told her audience on national television that I had bribed Eric and faked his conversion to Christ. She also accused me of faking Eric's marriage to Sondra.

I called ABC in New York and spoke for 90 minutes with a Miss Sutherland, who was one of the producers of Prime Time Live. I explained every detail of Eric's conversion, and told her how he had been forced to move out of San Francisco because of death threats. In this vulnerable time of transition, I had helped Eric with $500.00 a month for an apartment near Jubilee, where he attended church regularly. Someone else had given Eric an old car to help him with transportation.

"Thank you Pastor, for enlightening us," said Miss Sutherland.

But the show itself reflected otherwise. During the first 20 minutes Diane went after a preacher named W. V. Grant, Jr. I had barely heard of him, but I had to admit her story was very convincing. The next segment featured Larry Lea and also mentioned me. I couldn't believe what I saw. Lies, half-truths, and gross exaggerations. My blood hit the boiling point when Sawyer portrayed Eric living in an expensive condo on a golf course. She said I'd wined and dined him so that he would cooperate. The truth was that Carla and I *coffee'd* and *nacho'd* him as we'd shared Christ with him

Diane is good. She comes across sincere and believable, but

so can Satan himself. I recognized in her cool vehemence that the world does hate Jesus and those who follow Him.

"Honey, she's lost and blind," Carla reminded me. "She thinks she's doing good. Just pray for her."

The next Sunday, Prime Time cameras came to Jubilee. The sheep were a little nervous. During my sermon time I answered every question raised by the telecast, and brought out the facts of Eric's conversion. The cameras rolled, but Diane never televised my rebuttal. I wonder why?

Did people leave the church over the Prime Time program? A few did, but not many. Actually, our congregation grew stronger through the ordeal. Thank God!

CHAPTER 10

INDIA RE-LOADED – TEN YEARS LATER

I returned to India 10 years later to hold my first crusade in GUNTUR, a city eight hours south of CHENNAI (formerly Madras), the capital city of Andhra Pradesh.

I was first introduced to American missionary Scott Norling and his work in India through the missionary efforts of my former secretary Virginia Obregon and her husband, George. In 1990, they had deployed to India to work alongside Scott and Melody Norling to preach in open-air crusades at several locations that Scott had pre-arranged. India is where they met the Norlings for the first time, having made a prior connection with his ministry, *Church on the Move*, based in Minnesota. When they were returning by rail from *Warangal*, Virginia ended her conversation with Scott: "I want to tell my pastor about your terrific work here in India, you need to connect with him; but I'm not promising you anything."

My return to India with Scott Norling was the beginning of a magnificent relationship that continues to this day. Unbeknownst to my secretary or me, Scott is a personal friend of Gayland, who you may recall was my travel companion and preaching partner in Guntur in 1992. They are both from Minnesota. The Norlings came into the picture through unrelated events and people in the States, yet while living in India. Virginia doesn't know Gayland. That is nothing short of amazing!

Scott is a man of many talents. He coordinates television broadcasting for Joyce Meyer's *Life in the Word* program in India, along with coordinating the humanitarian efforts of Franklin Graham's *Samaritan's Purse* and Pat Robertson's *Operation Blessing*. He also promoted crusades for T. L. Osborne, Reinhardt Bonnke and the late John Osteen. Scott Norling is a well-traveled man but more than that, he has a love and passion for India, the country he and his family have lived in for over a decade.

India has the largest television audience in the world. Scott's use of this mass media reached a milestone with the broadcast of my television program, *Jubilee,* which is aired in 9 different languages on 11 different television networks. Because many are bound by idolatry, superstition, and addictions, hearing these broadcasts in their own vernacular languages the Indian audience gets an instant connection with the messages.

As a result, every month Scott receives over 10,000 letters from viewers – but within 48 hours each one is mailed a gospel booklet in their own language. Then, every month Scott holds dozens of meetings in different cities where these viewers are invited for a time of worship, testimonies, and instruction. Local churches are then given their names for further follow-up.

 SOURCE OF DISEASE ~ SOURCE OF LIFE

I'd forgotten how desperate and childlike Indians were. I felt like a real Christian walking among them, looking for ways to improve their village lives.

With the church's generosity in bringing me here, I took a drink from the first water well Scott had dug with the funds raised by Jubilee.

In India a primary source of disease is found in contaminated water. Scarcity of clean drinking water, and water-borne diseases are huge problems facing India. Nearly one million Indian children die of diarrheal diseases every year as a direct result of drinking unsafe water.

Although pure, clean, safe drinking water is a universal human need, I've discovered that in India, the struggle for water assumes dimensions that we can hardly grasp. Imagine walking 4 hours every day to get water. This is a reality across India. Now, it costs $1000.00 to dig a bore well with a hand pump, but each can serve an entire village. Once the water well is dug it becomes a huge source of life, and evangelizing the village can be easy.

I made a lifelong commitment to continue helping Indian villages with this life-giving project of providing water wells, medical supplies, and the Word of God. To date our church has helped dig scores of wells throughout South India.

Another source of life to Indians is *Bethel Bible College.* With our financial help, Bethel Bible College was started in Guntur, in Andhra Pradesh State to meet the vital need of training workers to bring in the vast Indian harvest. For students who have completed a high school education, Bethel offers a one and two-year certificate program taught in the local language of *Telegu.* For those with an undergraduate degree, Bethel offers a Master of Divinity, taught in English. Students completing either of these courses are well trained for work as village and town pastors, evangelists, and church planters.

Children are at the heart of God's Kingdom. Studies indicate that 80 percent of all people who accept Christ do so before the age of 15. In India 18 million children have to work for a living, some from as young as the age of five. They are virtual slaves in a free land; millions more live on the streets where they are orphans, homeless, or simply abandoned.

Fortunately, over the last several years, Scott and Melody, with the help of other donors like our church, have established 14 children's homes in different parts of India. These homes provide a godly, safe environment and provide for the children's spiritual, physical and emotional needs. Clothes, meals and food expenses are all paid for, including the homes' operating costs.

These fortunate children are learning about the love of God in word and deed, and have hope for living a happy, normal life.

> *Whoever welcomes a child in my name, welcomes*
> *Me.* ~MATTHEW 18:5

CHURCH PLANTING AND CRUSADES

There is nothing quite like mass crusades that result in the miracle of salvation. Through crusade evangelism, literally tens-of-thousands not only hear the Gospel but also experience God's wonder-working miracles. Scott and I have partnered together in the last several years to carry out crusades in *Hyderabad, Chennai, Mumbai, Bangalore, Vizag,* and *Guntur.* But, the 1995 crusade in Hyderabad topped them all.

Before I share the phenomenal success of that Jubilee mission crusade I want to share an excerpt of a unique prophecy given to Carla and me by Dr. Myles Munroe in August of 1995. The prophetic word he gave us marked the beginning of a new course for Jubilee:

> *"Pastor Dick, God is going to give you a completely new experience in India this time. It's not going to be like all the others. This one is different. You are going to hear information when he comes back from India that he was never able to tell you before.*
>
> *But God is going to give this man, tonight, a ministry that is going to be twice the depth of the Third World countries than he has had before. India is going to respond to you like never before. It is going to be as though all the previous trips were like visits. This one is a mission. Third-World anointing. Thank you Father."*

This was my 4th missionary crusade to India. This crusade in the city of Hyderabad lasted 6 nights, with 1.7 million people gathering to hear the Gospel message. The Hyderabad crusade caught national attention and was shown all over India on the evening news. More than 800,000 individuals received Christ as their Lord and Savior. Unfortunately, we only had 50,000 Bibles to pass out to new converts. That week the *Hindu Daily News* reported that we had *"the largest gathering of humanity in the history of India to hear the gospel preached."* Another reporter wrote, *"Even Gandhi himself never drew such a crowd."* I even found myself stuck in traffic for over an hour-and-a-half as 20 percent of the city came to our gospel crusade.

Operation Bangalore - The planning and preparation that led up to our crusade in October of 1997 nearly wasn't enough for what we encountered! The opposition was so great we almost threw in the towel. My crusade team had arrived early only to find that the land we secured six months earlier had been denied access by the State Supreme Court in *Karnataka*. Only in India could they do this to us.

As Scott relayed the account blow by blow, I clenched the phone in my fist and found a few feeble words to eke out, "What now?" I asked.

He informed me that we had one final chance to approach the court to state our case, or we could fax all our guest speakers coming for the crusade and tell them not to come since alternative sites were unsuitable for the event.

I said, "Let's go forward."

I must admit it wasn't a very forceful charge. I knew God could work miracles but at 3:00 a.m. and with such devastating news, I was flabbergasted.

My wife and I began praying. We called every prayer warrior we knew to pray and my faith began to rise again. We stood our ground in prayer and waited for his phone call. Scott called and said that the judge's ruling was still *NO*.

Then, and I'm not being one bit theatrical, according to Scott, a Hindu woman lawyer who was in court for another case stopped the judge as he was on his way out and asked why he didn't grant the land. The judge was astonished that someone would question his decision, and would even attempt to approach him when court was over. That was just not done.

He turned and ridiculed her and asked what business it was

of hers. She stood stronger and became bolder. *She was being used by the Lord to speak on our behalf.* After several verbal exchanges the judge turned and said, "Okay, Okay, have the land, but it will cost you $10,000 extra for the cleanup and repair of the property."

The team stood totally astonished. They had just witnessed a miracle. God heard the cries of His people and answered!

We packed our bags and headed for India, making sure to bring our mosquito spray for those pesky mosquitoes that come out at night during the crusades.

We were pretty excited after our major victory. Crowds poured in each night to hear the anointed worship of Ron Kenoly, and powerful preaching by my guests that included Marilyn Hickey, Ulf Ekman, my son Adam, and Steve Hage. When Marilyn went to the platform to speak, some of the men left. I didn't care because I wanted her there to prove that women can minister. That night 120,000 gave their lives to Christ. Ron Kenoly's concert style presentation was revolutionary and ministered to the thousands present. Ours was the second ever gospel crusade and youth rally in *Bangalore.*

Several weeks later after returning from Bangalore we received a phone call from Scott Norling telling us that while we were there, he received serious bomb threats that were directed at the team and the crusade grounds. Scott had a prayer team assembled to cover the Jubilee team and event and didn't want to alarm us. Boy, that was living life on the edge...

In February of 2001, M.C. Hammer joined us in *Mumbai* to do a gospel concert and youth rally, partnering with *Pepsi Cola* and *MTV*. There were 20,000 in attendance every night and the concert was well received by our East Indian friends.

In February of 2002, I assisted Dr. Cho with ministry in Puna, India as thousands of leaders gathered to receive instruction and encouragement to carry on their work in this vast nation. Much of Dr. Cho's India ministry schedule has now been delegated to me because as he gets older he is cutting back on his travels. I say this as a matter of fact, but it is truly a privilege to fill in for Dr. Cho. The fact that he would find me suitable for the job is encouraging.

In February of 2003, with a pastoral team from Jubilee, we held two Government of 12 (G-12) conferences, one in Mumbai and one in Chennai. Over 11,500 leaders attended to learn about this innovative approach to ministry based on Jesus' discipling His twelve who were chosen to carry the Gospel to the world.

At this writing, Scott negotiated a television contract with *Zee-TV* to air our programs to reach now over a billion people in India, including surrounding countries such as Pakistan, parts of China, and Indonesia.

In late 2004, I plan to return to *VISHAKHAPATNAM* for a weeklong crusade where 250,000 are expected to attend. In conjunction with the crusade schedule we will also be training 5,000 pastors in the G-12 cell vision.

Years ago when the Lord spoke to me and declared,

"You are called to this nation,"

I decided that I would not let my church be left in comfortable ignorance about India *or* about God's Great Commission.

How much of our work will endure, the future will disclose. The people of India worship 300 million gods. When I scan the human landscape of India's poor, it's amazing to me how idols keep these desperately poor deceived, —they're nothing more than prisoners of their gods!

But I know that my Gospel is India's hope!

Part Four

The Kingdom Is Within

The kingdom of God

does not come with observation;

nor will they say, 'See here!

or See there!' For indeed,

the kingdom of God is within you.

-*Luke 17:20-21*

Chapter 11

Time For a Release

A fresh positive feeling continued to infuse Jubilee Christian Center. Attendance soared and we were having 3 Sunday morning services and numerous programs and ministries throughout the week. Our 15-member band and lively red-robed choir really rocked in worship and praise. Offerings continued to rise, so that we could begin making plans to finally design a sanctuary of our own.

In the spring of 1993, Carla and I were invited to Johannesburg, South Africa for the first time to preach for a dear friend and C.G.I. Board Member, Theo Wolmarans. Apartheid was the major headlines in the press at the time, and tensions were high. South African apartheid, by law, segregated the whites from non-whites in all aspects of life. For example, blacks were prohibited from holding many jobs, and were not allowed to run businesses or professional practices in any areas designated as being for whites only. I did my best to teach on racial reconciliation which I knew wasn't falling on deaf ears.

We visited South Africa three months before Nelson Mandela was sworn in as President of the country. The first thing he did while in office was to set up the Truth and Reconciliation Commission and to rewrite the Constitution. Mandela terminated the apartheid era, but the legacy of apartheid and the social imbalances it engendered will take decades for all African nationals to unlearn. There were racial tensions before we left and when I returned with Dr. Cho years later.

I really admired multi-racial churches there that have weathered the storms, preaching Christ more than preaching nationalism.

TRAVELOGUE: *KRUGER NATIONAL PARK*

After our ministry time at the church, the Wolmarans invited us to a safari at the Kruger National Park. To this day, Carla and I agree it was the highlight vacation of our lives.

I could hardly sleep the night before imagining what this adventure would bring. Donning safari attire early the next morning, we made our departure for *Lion Sands Private Game Reserve,* which is situated in one of the finest wilderness areas in the Southern Kruger Park region. It is roughly the size of Massachusetts. Driving into the game reserve our eyes were quickly absorbed by the roaming wildlife and unspoiled landscape that passed before us.

We anxiously unpacked and settled into the game lodge that afternoon, ready for action. Our guide carefully planned our schedule to make sure we made the most of our time in the bush, encouraging us to watch for the hunter's "big five"- elephant, buffalo, rhino, lion, and the elusive leopard. From an information-filled bush walk, to game spotting in a chauffer-driven open safari 4-wheel-drive, we were literally surrounded by a spectacular array of wildlife and nature for hundreds of miles in every direction; it was surreal.

A full day of game driving included outings at dawn when the animals are most active and in the late morning and afternoon when the natural setting was right for picture taking. Carla and I were like two excited little kids pointing out to each other the exotic array of birds, the tigers, rhino, and antelope. We drove to the edge of the lake and viewed the vast game herds that gathered to drink and bathe while they stayed alert to the lions close by in the grass, the leopards in the trees, and the giant crocodiles. Water holes dotted the landscape and were some of the most interesting spots to watch these animals in their natural habitat.

By nature I am an ardent hunter and outdoorsman. But, somehow I didn't feel like hunting. My instinct for hunting was subdued by the beauty and wonder of my surroundings.

Our routine mornings began at 5:30 a.m. exploring God's creation, and we didn't turn in until late at night, listening to the nocturnal wildlife come alive. The beauty of a family gathering of lions taking it easy on the roadside in their natural setting was nothing short of majestic. As we continued our drive over a well-driven path, we spotted an elegant zebra at a distance on the lookout for danger. At one point, our driver was forced to stop when several giraffe stepped in front of our vehicle to cross our path – our jaws dropped. We whipped out our camera, removed the shutter and started squeezing rounds of photos. I was waiting for one of the giraffes to crane its long neck down to greet us, but they didn't appear to be phased by all the excitement going on around them.

Looking up into a shady tree we were coming upon we almost missed a cheetah draping lazily over a huge tree limb taking an afternoon nap. We were careful not to disturb him.

We spotted Africa's "river horse" – rotund hippos loitering in a shallow watering hole. Herds of impalas, gazelles and African buffalo were resting in the afternoon sun. Finally, we captured a glimpse of stampeding elephants on the horizon – as a group of lions drew upon them by surprise, spooking them – leaving a cloud of dust trailing behind.

"Look for the warthogs and waterbucks," our tour guide prompted as we were leaving the park to return to Johannesburg for our departure to the States. It was sure a bittersweet farewell.

I never thought in my wildest imaginations that I would go on a safari. I used to watch *Animal Kingdom* and *Tarzan* on television as a boy growing up, but never thought I would take in the experience of being up close with God's majestic creation in Africa. The thrill of this adventure was nothing short of extraordinary!

MURIEL 'TUDY' HAYES

Tudy was the name my mother, Muriel, was fondly known by. Mom and Emmett were living on Angel's Landing Road in Prunedale, California during this time, enjoying their peaceful life away from the big city life of San Jose. Mom was a strong, vibrant woman who became more nostalgic in her later years, and enjoyed the company of her family, especially her grandkids.

One afternoon my sister Judy called me concerned for Mom, sensing something was wrong. "Dick, she doesn't sound good, I'll call you later and let you know how she's doing after I take her to the doctor," Judy instructed.

When Emmett and Judy took Mom to the hospital, the doctor gave the diagnosis; Mom had lung cancer that was quickly spreading to her brain. The doctors didn't give her long to live. Emmett had a hard time caring for Mom, watching her health rapidly deteriorate and needed help. Ed and Juanita were busy pastoring a church in Morgan Hill, so Judy moved in with Mom and Emmett to care for her during this time.

I wasn't ready to see Mom in the throes of cancer, wanting to remember her as she was before this fatal illness. Knowing the volatile condition Mom was in though, we knew we needed to pay her a visit. We drove up to the familiar little white house my Mom and step-Dad had built and not a thing was out of place. Walking past the front gate, I noticed her vegetable garden, the roses were in full bloom, and a variety of flowers brightened the yard. Mom had become an avid gardener and enjoyed working outdoors. She was also an artist and her many paintings reflected her love of gardening.

I opened the screen door and immediately noticed Mom sitting in an over-stuffed chair in the family room with a quilted blanket laid across her lap.She was still able to recognize us but did very little talking. We spent the day visiting, feeling a bit awkward under the circumstances but we made the best of our time together, praying for Mom before we left. She extended her delicate hands embracing mine and smiled, thanking us for coming. I bent over to kiss her cheek, staring at her soft hazel eyes and hugged her gently, "I love you, Mom," aware that she didn't have much longer to live. That was the last time we would see Mom alive. The road back home was long and contemplating.

I called Judy later that week to see how Mom was doing.

"Judy," I said, "I feel somewhat guilty that we haven't spent much time with Mom." In a calm, reassuring way Judy said, "Dick, Mom wouldn't recognize you anyway; besides, she doesn't want anyone to see her in this condition."

On July 12, 1993, Mom passed away. She wasn't one for elaborate events, so Judy took care of the details of the burial. Afterwards, we had a big family gathering, a memorial of sorts, at Ed and Juanita's house, and shared the wonderful memories of a life that meant so much to so many. As we were closing, we gathered in a circle to pray and as I cleared my throat I could hardly hold back the flood of emotions as we released Mom to God's care and prayed for Emmett who had just lost his best friend.

For many years during Christmas Eve, the entire family spent it at Mom's place. She and grandma would cook up our favorite roasted turkey and homemade Rocky Road candy. With all the fixin's of an old fashioned traditional Christmas, we enjoyed each other's company, making memories around the fireplace listening to *Bing Crosby* and *Frank Sinatra* run through a bumper crop of old favorites. To listen to these two American legends duet on "White Christmas," I guess that's why I love the Christmas season so much.

￬

Good friend and prophet, Kim Clement, came to minister in March of 1994 and spoke the word of the Lord to me during the service:

> *"For the Lord says I am going to grant unto you*
> *that very thing that they said is impossible. For I*
> *am going to give you a building, says God, and a*

place that is so vast that many will flock to the place and will say, 'Let us go to the house of the Lord and let us rejoice.'...I am not going to give you one building, I am going to give you three different buildings... In the next few months there is going to be miraculous provision, says the Lord."

I have received many prophetic words throughout my life, some more stirring and direct than others. Yet, I was always left to wonder just what those words really meant and exactly how they would come to pass.

It's about Providence.

A GODSEND

One day in June of 1994, a church member named Carl Story called me and said, "Pastor, meet me at my lawyer's office tomorrow."

"Sure, Carl, what's up?"

Without answering, Carl suggested that I bring Dr. Kim too. The next day we sat around the lawyer's conference room, when Carl broke into a big smile. "Pastor," he asked, "how do you want the stock made out; to you personally or to the church?" He was talking about 1.5 million shares of a Silicon Valley high tech company ready to go on the NASDAQ Board.

"Uh, make it out to Jubilee, Carl." I winked at Dr. Kim.

Whew, I passed the temptation test!

Shortly afterwards, we sold the stock for $4.2 million. Bless his heart, Carl moved on to find other Christian ministries to help.

Wherever you are Carl Story, thank you. You were a god-send.

> *Eye has not seen, nor ear heard, nor have entered into the heart of man the things which God has prepared for those who love Him.* ~1 CORINTHIANS 2:9

MY PERSONAL JUBILEE!

I turned 50 October 30, 1994. Me, 50! - Unbelievable, but true. In the Old Testament the year of Jubilee meant the year of release. All debts were forgiven and all slaves were freed. It happened every 50 years. Pentecost also means "50" and in the New Testament it represents the outpouring of the Holy Spirit on all flesh - plenty there to be happy about.

My 50th birthday was special. Oral Roberts preached the Sunday morning service and touched our hearts. My Christian publisher friend Stephen Strang was in town for a visit. Ken Norton, Sr., sent me a pair of boxing gloves with *"Happy Birthday"* written on each glove. And Merton Hanks, all-pro safety for the San Francisco 49ers, showed up at my party and gave me a football signed by the Super Bowl championship team of 1994-1995.

They even brought the *Batmobile* up from Los Angeles for me to drive around the hotel parking lot. It was a great time. I felt alive and confident once more. Carla and I were like two high school kids in love. Life was sweet.

During this time a well-known evangelist friend from Texas was in town and I received a great revelation about my life. He shared a recent self-discovery. He said he had lived a shame-based life for many years, always wanting to live up to his father's expectations, yet always falling short. This struck a chord deep within me.

He asked, "Dick, ever hear the story of the great London fire a few centuries back?" I had but the details were sketchy.

"During those years there was a horrible black plague that devastated a good part of Europe. No one could figure out what brought it on every spring. And then the worst fire in London's history nearly wiped out the city. It was devastating."

"Spring arrived," he continued, "and no plague; folks were relieved, but puzzled. As the clean-up of the city began, the workers went down into the sewers of London and found piles of dead rats killed by the fire. And millions and millions of dead fleas. The fire killed not only the rats but the plague-carrying fleas."

"Pastor," my friend continued, "shame is nothing more than spiritual rats and plaque - carrying fleas. The fire of the baptism of the Holy Spirit is the only thing that can get down into the sewers of our souls. God is giving me that fire John the Baptist spoke of and I'm being set free from shame. Pastor Dick, I think you need a dose of Holy Ghost fire yourself."

"Amen, brother," I sighed.

That Friday night as my friend preached at our church I asked God to send the fire. He did! It was painful as the spirit of God went deep down into my life, my past pain, shame, and guilt, and began to burn up the rats and plague-infested fleas.

As this happened I received a fresh revelation of God as my Father. I had always struggled for a picture of God the Father. I felt more comfortable with Jesus as my Lord. Jesus was a construction worker, so was I. Jesus liked to fish, so did I. Jesus hung out with the boys, so did I. Jesus wasn't afraid of anyone, nor was I. I liked Jesus, and the Holy Spirit was becoming a real friend and helper.

In my prayer time I would talk to Jesus and the Holy Spirit, but felt anxious addressing the Father. *Why get too close to Father God?* I reasoned. *Maybe He too will leave me.* I remember as a seven-year-old waiting for 8 hours out in front of the house for my father to pick me up to go fishing. He had promised the week before, on one of his rare visits, to take me to the lake and teach me how to catch bluegill. He must have gotten drunk or just plain forgot. I waited and waited. Putting my stuff away in the garage I remember thinking, *Fathers just can't be trusted. Oh well, I still have Grandma, Mom and my sisters. That's enough for me.*

Amazing how young memories last so long. But, here I was in 1994 during my 50th birthday party finally seeing my Heavenly Father in a new way; my real Father; father to the fatherless, a friend to those in need. The Father dwells within us and it is His good pleasure to give us the kingdom.

> *Do not fear, little flock, for it is your Father's good pleasure to give you the kingdom.* ~LUKE 12:32

Ron Kenoly was now gaining notoriety in the Christian music arena, working with Mike Coleman and Don Moen of Integrity Music. Stephen Strang and John Mason from Creation House Publishers approached Ron and me with the idea of partnering together to write a practical guide to praise and worship. We were able to integrate our leadership experiences to provide a balanced view of how these roles can and should interact together. The book is entitled, *Lifting Him Up*.

ANOTHER WORD OF PROPHECY

As previously mentioned, in August of 1995, Dr. Myles Munroe ministered a prophetic word to Carla and me regarding India. But another portion of that prophecy included the following:

> *Your pastor has been carrying a lot of burdens in regards to the future of this ministry. There is a great dream in his heart. I don't know him well, but I know a vision when I see one. He's got one! He's going to be a new man tonight!*
>
> *God is going to give you a breakthrough in your building. He is going to give you a breakthrough in your media ministry... He is going to give you a breakthrough in the expansion of the work in the Valley.*
>
> *God is going to give you the establishment of a couple of other new churches out of this work in the next couple of years. People are going to leave this church sent out to start other works.*

Words of encouragement continued to come in and they became a source of great comfort to us in the midst of the battles we would soon face with our new building project.

We made the decision in January to pay off the 10 acres

across the street that would hold our new sanctuary. Our vision to reach the world through missions and through media took greater shape in 1996. Jubilee was now seen in 3 million homes in the Bay Area through our local Sunday morning television broadcasts. Our television department also launched into international markets and was carried a good part of the year on the *Inspirational Network* and in India.

MARCH FOR JESUS - JERUSALEM

My chest itched like crazy after the 24-hour journey to Jerusalem. In my hotel I had jet lag and just couldn't sleep.

Carla and I had traveled to Jerusalem for a Church Growth International Conference early in the spring of 1996. Dr. David Yonggi Cho organized the trip and appointed our church to capture this historic event on film. I brought our television crew to help me with this task. Dr. Robert Schuller would be the keynote speaker. Our purpose was to assemble 10,000 church leaders from throughout the world to honor the 2,000th birthday of Christ, and the 3,000th anniversary of King David's liberation of Jerusalem from the Jebusites. I had looked very much forward to being here, and now I was exhausted.

The following day we began a series of teachings and group visits to historic sites. I felt awe in the Garden of Gethsemane, recalling how Jesus fell down here in dreadful agony, and nobody stayed up the night to pray with Him. The Mount of Olives gave me a peaceful feeling. I wondered if some of these ancient olive trees had been here when Jesus walked through here.

We launched out in a small boat to film the Sea of Galilee.

At first the water was calm, but a good distance from the bank a sudden storm came up and I found out in a hurry exactly how scared the disciples must have felt. Within minutes the waves were almost capsizing our boat. Our cameraman lurched sideways, almost falling out of the boat, and while grabbing for the camera I smacked my head against the lens. In the documentary video that we made, a scab under my left eye is visible!

On the last day we staged our climactic March for Jesus. The government gave us special permission to march from the Jerusalem Conference Center to the Knesset Parliament, a first for Christians. Soldiers were posted on route to make sure there were no incidents. Not everyone was happy that we were there.

Carla and I, together with the camera crew, helped lead the parade of 10,000 Christians dressed in the traditional dress of their countries from all over the world. We sang hymns and gospel songs. The atmosphere was charged with excitement as we celebrated the 2000th birthday of the King of Kings, in the city of His resurrection! Truly, we experienced the power of the Holy Spirit to anoint people in reconciliation and joy.

On the final day, Dr. Cho addressed the conference members. He said, "The fulfillment of Jesus Christ's commandment 2000 years ago to go into all the world and preach the gospel was manifested as saints from many countries have come to celebrate His coming into the world."

BE INSTANT IN SEASON AND OUT

Then came time for Dr. Robert Schuller to give the closing address. But there was a hitch. He had to leave sooner than expected to catch a flight. And suddenly I was asked to fill in the gap. I didn't have time to think because Dr. Schuller was already speaking.

"What shall we give Jesus for His birthday?" he asked the huge crowd. "Let's give Him our lives so filled with the Holy Spirit that we will honor His name." A chorus of praise welled up from the delegates as thousands of arms were raised toward heaven.

After he finished his remarks, Dr. Schuller was ushered out to catch his plane. I looked out at the delegates. Not only was I following a tough act, I felt intimidated by my peers in the audience.

I had a fleeting thought to try and preach my best sermon, but this left me, and instead I whispered a desperate prayer: *"God, You're going to have to help me. I'm dry as the Sahara desert, and tired. I thought I was here on a spiritual vacation. I can't make the switch. Anoint me, please."*

I asked myself what Jesus would do if He was here celebrating with us. The answer came*: touch them in their point of deepest need.* Suddenly I was overwhelmed by the reality that there were needy people out there. People didn't want a sermon, they wanted ministry. Everyone needs ministering, even those living successful Christian lives!

So I talked about the comfort and renewal that arises from the kingdom of God, and then gave an altar call. I was astonished to see several hundred come down. I prayed with each one for their individual need. One by one people left until I was standing alone with my cameraman. Though tired and weak, feeling the effects of shingles, I had served the Lord to the best of my ability.

But those who wait on the Lord shall renew their strength; they shall mount up with wings like eagles, they shall run and not be weary, they shall walk and not faint. ~ISAIAH 40:31

God again revealed that the more helpless and yielded I am to Him, the more He can work through me. What if I had been told ahead of time that I was supposed to speak to this distinguished crowd of Christians? I would have researched for days, poured over notes, and made sure my sermon was the most impressive that I could come up with.

But that was not what God had in mind for these people. He knew their greatest need. I did not. It's funny how God, by keeping me off my stride, actually lets me find my stride, lets me do the best I can. As the Lord said to Paul, "My grace is sufficient for thee: for my strength is made perfect in weakness" (II Corinthians 12:9), and that is successful Christian living!

OUR NEW 3,500-SEAT SANCTUARY

No matter what blows the devil dishes out or what Jesus asks us to do, we can rest assured that the kingdom of God is within us. Thank God that my dear wife Carla has this conviction and continues to claim victory even *before* the outcome has materialized.

Days from breaking ground for our new sanctuary – that would seat 3,500 – everyone was excited and I was energized and thrilled. I then received bad news. The U.S. Army Corps of Engineers wanted to turn our building site into a marsh for ducks. They red-flagged the property and claimed that we had dropped the permit process and that blue flowers were now growing on the property. They now wanted to label the property as *wetlands*. The government didn't want us to build a church sanctuary on the site —but we had paid off the $5 million dollar, 10-acre parcel in 1996!

"My God," I thought, *"me battling the devil and the U.S. government?"* But my wife clearly grasped the situation and declared, "Dick, everything is okay! Honey, the battle is the Lord's – and He's already won."

Although our building program was a time of great frustration for me, I pressed on and stayed the course. I was continually reminded of the words prophesied over us by Kim Clement and Myles Munroe and this helped me to stay the course.

My brother-in-law Ed wasn't going to budge either. The prayers of the saints were covering us the whole time.

By God's grace we received favorable treatment in the matter. I would later discover that the Commander of the Army Corps of Engineers assigned to us, a 70-year-old engineer, whose call it was to either grant or deny permission to build, was a short-timer. He was resigning from his government post Friday of that week. Between our attorneys, by brother-in-law Ed and the Army Corps of Engineers they went at it and finally we prevailed. The last official act he performed at his post in the San Francisco District – was to sign-off on our permits to begin construction on our new sanctuary.

I was in London with Morris Cerullo and Benny Hinn when my secretary faxed the news that we were granted the permits to build. I was ecstatic because I knew the Army Corps of Engineers could be worse than the I.R.S. in their dealings with citizens.

In July of 1997, with government approval in hand, we held a Groundbreaking Ceremony on site.

Amidst the chemotherapy, radiation, pain pills, and frustration, Ed's determination and strong will to get Jubilee built was inspirational. He had been diagnosed with cancer in 1992 and was given 90 days-to-12 months to live, but he hung on. He was so focused on getting the sanctuary built that he willed himself to live for another five years. Ed had a drive in him that wouldn't stop. Everyday he went to the construction site to monitor the progress of the crew. The walls were being poured and hoisted into position, nearing completion of the exterior of the building. Juanita recalls one of the construction crew telling her that they were watching Ed one morning as he slowly circled the building examining the structure in a very peculiar way.

"Somehow I knew he was saying goodbye, knowing that his job was done," Juanita somberly reflected.

Two days later, November 11, 1997, Ed passed onto glory.

Juanita asked Ed prior to his death that day about finishing the rest of the building. Ed's reply was simply, "Send me a post card when it's finished."

Seven months later we completed construction of the new sanctuary and it was near time to celebrate!

But, before doing so we were off to Rio de Janeiro, Brazil.

⌣

Both Carla and I made our way to Rio where hundreds of pastors were scheduled to attend the very first spiritual warfare conference, as the local pastors billed it. It was wintertime and the weather was wonderful. Ron Kenoly joined us to do praise and worship, and other close friends arrived to help minister to the pastors. We were able to have my book *Curses* translated in the Portuguese language to make it available to the pastors, along with my audio and video series, *"Breaking Strongholds."*

Our host, Pastor Marco Peixoto, whom I believe is the spiritual gatekeeper in Rio and who is being used mightily there, already has one of the largest churches in Rio. While there, Pastor Marco, our interpreter Jim Pope, and I went to the famous Christ statue that overlooks Rio, high atop a mountain, and we interceded in prayer for the city. It was an incredible experience.

SANCTUARY GRAND OPENING

As one can well imagine I was like a kid in front of a candy store anxiously waiting for the shop owner to open the store so I could run in and fill my pockets with goodies knowing my dad was going to pay the bill. Weeks and months of planning for this event pumped me with unimaginable excitement. It reminded me of the movie *Field of Dreams* – "If you build it, they will come."

On June 19, 1998 we celebrated the grand opening of our new sanctuary. This was without a doubt, a turning point in my life and the future of this ministry.

Join me as I recapture highlights of the Grand Opening-Dedication of our state-of-the-art sanctuary, media, and world outreach center. This 80,000 square foot sanctuary also houses a bookstore, early childhood ministry, choir room, multi-purpose room and kitchen; all under one roof.

The pomp of the occasion reminded me of King Solomon and how he must have felt when he had completed the temple his father King David had begun prior to his death. *"So all the work that King Solomon had done for the house of the Lord was finished; and Solomon brought in the things which his father David had dedicated; the silver and the gold and the furnishings. He put them in the treasuries of the house of the Lord"* (1 Kings 7:51). Once the temple was completed and the ark of the covenant was in place, King Solomon held an elaborate ceremony dedicating the temple to the Lord.

Acknowledging the people who have been instrumental in bringing this vision to pass, my brother-in-law, the late Pastor Ed Pearson was first on my list. He meant so much to me, especially while he was battling cancer in the planning and construction phase of the church.

Those who attended the ceremony were friends from all walks of life – government officials, sports personalities, ministers and many others, who came to celebrate what the Lord had done.

My first associate, Pastor Richard Cardoza quoted the late Dr. Sumrall saying, "You aren't really a church until you are at least 10-years-old and you've been through two to three staffs." This statement rang true for us.

My first pastor from Paradise Christian Center, Pastor Vince O'Shaughnessy, conveyed his heartfelt congratulations in his distinctive Irish brogue with, *"Baby, you've come a long way."*

During the ceremony my dear friend Dr. Jim Reeve reminded us of a placard he saw one day in front of a church building situated in the English countryside: "In the year 1653 when all things sacred in the kingdom were profaned and defiled this church was built to do the best of things in the worst of times." Jim declared, "Jubilee was built to do the best of things in the worst of times."

To further celebrate this historic achievement, we watched video greetings on our large television screens from various ministry friends and government officials that weren't able to attend. The words of encouragement and enthusiasm added to the event like the icing on a chocolate cake. It sure is good to have friends.

Dr. Cho spoke prophetic words that are still coming to pass today,

> *"God has blessed you peculiarly! God has raised up this church for this generation. God has laid out this foundation for you to carry the glory of our Lord Jesus Christ and to bring the kingdom to the ends of the earth."*

I was truly astounded...

My Canadian friends, Pastor Cal and Jan Switzer affirmed the words of the Apostle Paul to the Romans, "Your faith and great works are talked about all over the world."

Pastor John Kilpatrick who pastored the Pensacola revival declared to me, "Dick, you have always been on the cutting edge of what God is doing and saying. I believe that the next few years are going to be Jubilee years for you and your church."

We were all reminded of a critical time in American History when President Abraham Lincoln wrote the Emancipation Proclamation. It was a wake-up call that set into motion unprecedented changes that would free slaves from bondage and bring equality to the races. Later, Dr. Martin Luther King's noteworthy speech, *"I Have a Dream"* was certainly a plea for liberty among the races – African-Americans, Asians, Native Americans, and Caucasians. But some 2,000 years ago a greater *Emancipation Proclamation* was written and signed in the blood of Jesus declaring we've been set free, and we have a message of liberty to tell the world.

An observation often quoted by King is still true today: the most segregated time of the week is 11:00 a.m. on Sunday. While it is true that some are catching the vision of integration, like Jubilee, ethnic churches are still a magnetic force. In order for a community to get to a higher level of racial reconciliation we need more churches to straddle the divide. More importantly, a heart change is necessary for genuine unity to occur. For there is neither Jew nor Greek, neither slave nor free, male nor female, for we all are all one in Christ Jesus, according to Galatians 3:28.

We are called to be an earthly expression of God's love for "every nation, tribe, language and people" (Revelation 14:6). It is the church's responsibility to help the nation heal from racial divisiveness. Our church represents a diversity of races all worshipping together. Being racially diverse has caused many to be drawn to our church.

My friend and neighbor to the east of Jubilee, Pastor Willie Gains of Emmanuel Baptist Church, showed his support encouraging us with the profound words *Mordecai* spoke to *Queen Esther* before she approached the King for the salvation of her people, "God has brought you into the kingdom for such a time as this." Pastor Gains is African-American and we have both preached at each other's churches. Jubilee planted a financial seed to support his efforts when he was building his church. That's what friends are for.

Our celebration wouldn't have been complete without my dear friends, Mertin and Marva Hanks who had been Jubilee members for eight years. Developing a relationship with the Hanks was something that brought more opportunities for me to spread the gospel in the world of professional sports than I could have ever imagined. I have met and ministered to so many professional sports athletes, have spent time at the 49er's training camp and have met some coaches that were truly hungry for a gospel witness. NFL video greetings came from Coach Steve Mariucci, at the time coach of the 49er's, and his boss Carmen Policy. My having spent time with them I know I planted seeds of destiny into their lives.

Mike Hayes is one of my dearest friends in the world. If I could have had a brother to grow up and have fun with it would have been him because he's just a little crazier than I am. A man's man, Mike and his wife Kathy have been a support and great inspiration to Carla and me through the years. He and his wife pastor Covenant Faith Center in Carrolton, Texas, and they flew out to be with us to celebrate. Mike Hayes declared, "You are a 21st century ministry, Jubilee. You are not renters anymore you are land owners!"

In his overwhelming exuberance he gazed at Carla and me and said with conviction, "The glory of the latter house will be greater than the former. This is just the beginning. The best is yet to come – it is harvest time! You are impacting the Bay Area. A leader can dream but if he doesn't find people who will hitch their wagon to that star it will never happen."

How true that is. I began thinking about my staff and our Jubilee family and how they have been faithful throughout the years to support the vision the Lord gave me. I know I couldn't do this alone; it was and still is much too big for me.

At the close of this service, Pastor Mike and his wife Kathy, together with my other minister friends gathered around Carla and me and prayed for us. Their prayer spoke volumes to me:

> *"God raised them up for this time. They weren't born pastors. They are not 4th generation Pentecostals. Their dads were not pastors. God raised them up as a firebrand plucked out of the coals. They are arranged for this hour. Jubilee is poised for the next millennium."*

It was amazing for me to realize that beyond the frustration and anger and the battles we fought, something of great importance was revealed to me. My experiences to this point had taught me that we *overcame* and *prevailed:* against scandal, bad press, the Sierra Club, the Army Corps of Engineers, the devil, and others. Jesus is my faithful witness Who gave my actions compulsion to press on and to stay my course even when things looked very bleak. Indeed, our new Jubilee sanctuary is a testimony of overcoming faith.

As a result, Jubilee doubled in income and in people. Our new sanctuary became a magnet and as a result has attracted thousands of curious people through its doors to see just how the Lord intervened to bring about the miracle of Jubilee. In addition, our new media center allowed Jubilee to launch into live web-casting of our Sunday services on the Internet. We also began a weekly radio show in the Bay Area.

I felt like a heavyweight prizefighter the day after 15

rounds. Even though we were now in our new sanctuary I took a lot of blows. And, when you're in the fight you don't feel a lot of pain because your body pumps adrenaline during all the excitement. But the next day, when you wake up and your eye is shut, your lip is swollen, and ribs are broken, you realize, *"I won! —my God, look at me!"*

"Have I reached my high-water mark?" I asked myself. *"Should I slow down and simply teach, pastor the people, write books, and co-pastor with my son?"*

My Second Wind

At 54-years-old, and after 18 years of pastoring, I was worn out – *happy* – but exhausted.

But around this time I realized change was in the air and I began to get a second wind. It evolved in the following way.

I had met Colombian Pastor Cesar Castellanos through my friend Pastor Larry Stockstill, who invited me to his cell conference in Baton Rouge, Louisiana where Cesar and his wife Claudia Castellanos were speaking. I was attending the conference out of curiosity and to learn more about this G-12 concept of church life to see if this was the next direction for Jubilee. So, of course, the Castellanos' extended an invitation for us to see the vision in action.

Incredibly, after visiting the Castellanos' in Bogotá and observing the power of the G-12 cell system and experiencing my own personal encounter with the Lord, I felt "born-again" all over again, in a manner of speaking. Not only that, my notion of church cells involved adults and older people. But in Bogotá I witnessed two youth services attended by 45,000 young people. I saw thousands of young people animated with zeal for God, and felt their exuberant worship and hunger for God —*and many of them were in cells or were cell leaders*. I was awestruck. Bogotá easily dethroned my notion of who attends cells.

DEFINING THE GOVERNMENT OF 12

Cesar Castellanos' International Charismatic Mission (ICM) is the founding church of this strategy. They mushroomed from 70 small cell groups to 20,000 cells in just 18 years. Today, his church doesn't even count church members, only cells.

Castellanos studied how Jesus called twelve disciples knowing that the harvest was too plentiful for one man to reap. Jesus required others to help in ministering to the masses. So He began by mentoring twelve disciples. The multitudes followed the Master but He didn't train the multitudes. He only trained twelve. Castellanos pondered that if Jesus trained twelve —why should he minister any differently?

It's common knowledge that in a traditional church maybe 15 percent of the people are leaders, whereas in a cell church 100 percent are potential leaders because the cell church fosters that belief.

The G-12 cell system empowers people whereas traditional church leaves its people dependent on one person to do the pastoral work. A cell church is not just a church with cells. It is a place where the whole direction of the church's life and ministry takes place through the cells. Cells are not the same as home groups, fellowship groups or special interest groups.

Rather, they are tiny lively-stones, i.e. building blocks of church, while remaining part of the overall body.

⌣

Returning from Bogotá, Colombia, I realized how our church could go to the next level.

In 18 years we'd come this far just by being a program based, personality driven church. Now we're adapting to delegated leadership, i.e. shared leadership, where in the same tradition of John the Baptist, *Dick Bernal's* role must decrease so that my leaders may increase. The real heroes in this vision are the members of the church, not a handful of its super-sized leaders. Furthermore, in the same tradition of Jesus' ministry, I train and teach my disciples then send them out, deploying them under the spirit of the government of twelve. It is much more than a strategy or a method; it is a vision from the heart of the Father. The vision of the cells will provide not just numerical growth but a means of discipling and mobilizing the thousands within our church.

It takes hours to turn around an aircraft carrier in the water but it only takes a few seconds to turn around a speedboat; the difference of course is the size of the ship. Jubilee can be likened to an aircraft carrier, and Cesar Castellanos and I understood this and that is why he advised me to spend at least a year implementing the vision with my existing leaders and not to rock the boat with quick changes to the status quo.

That is what I did. I slowly baptized people in the G-12 vision to get church members talking about it. At my urging, many of my church staff visited Bogotá's revival and returned with renewed vision. I was glad they went to Bogotá because many weren't sure if the G-12 was just another one of my ideas that wouldn't last.

Later, when I finally implemented official changes to the requirements for church leadership (must be in a cell, or leading a cell) it was already a positive thing in most everyone's mind, and they saw it as something better.

Indeed, over a period of a year-and-a-half, I took my whole staff to Bogotá. And, just like the Hollywood movie TERMINATOR changed the way special effects were made, they, like me, saw for themselves the efficacy the *Encounters* and *School of Leaders* had on men's hearts and how it could forever change church for us.

It's also important to realize that when dealing with most people regarding change there are 3 gears of transition: slow, *slower*, and *slowest*. Although visionary people like myself hate redundancy and hate repeating ourselves we must learn how to because the people under us need constant repetition of revolutionary ideas in order to correctly carry them out.

To date, thousands of our church members have attended a Jubilee-sponsored three-day Encounter, and scores have enrolled and graduated from our School of Leaders. We now have over 450 cells throughout Silicon Valley. Our church is vibrant. The G-12 cell system has brushed complacency off Jubilee's body politic.

This has positively affected other churches, locally and abroad. Everyday, we get several calls from pastors in the U.S. wanting to know how they can transition to the government of 12 in their churches. Internationally, we have taken the G-12 concept to the pastors in India and the Philippines with fruitful results.

Cesar Castellanos received his mantle from Dr. David

Yonggi Cho and basically re-invigorated the mega-church cellular vision begun by Dr. Cho in the 1970s.

⌒

Through a mutual friend, long time back-up singer Ivory Stone, I invited legendary recording artist Smokey Robinson to minister at Jubilee. I grew up listing to Smokey's music and had heard that he gave his life to the Lord so I wanted him to share his testimony and sing at the church. When he came we spent some time together prior to the service, and instantly we hit it off. A couple of months later he called me and asked if I would help him do a Bible Study at his home, which I did once a month for three years.

That opportunity opened up doors for Carla and me to minister to a whole host of television celebrities, including Gary Busey, Judge Reinholt, Natalie Cole, Barry Gordy, and others. Smokey's my golfing buddy, but more than that he considers me one of his pastors.

〜 PRAY FOR THE BAY, SAN JOSE ARENA

On April 20, 1999, two students went on a shooting rampage at Columbine High School in Littleton, Colorado. Dylan Klebold, 18, and Eric Harris, 17, killed 12 students and one teacher before committing suicide. Our nation was consumed with what caused these boys to carry out a massacre that had been planned for over a year.

American teenagers live in a culture inundated with messages of death: movies, music, TV programs, and computer games are *saturated* with violence and random killings.

Shortly after the tragedy prophetess, Cindy Jacobs came to

our church and shared her thoughts on the tragedy, leading our church into a time of prayer. She was clearly moved to encourage the Bay Area to counter the attack by coming together, calling a solemn assembly to lift the fear from our children, parents, and teachers across the nation. As the Church and body of Christ, we have been given the authority over the enemy's assignments. The world doesn't have the power to make a difference in the hearts and minds of our society – we do! The word of the Lord through Cindy came as a clarion call and we had to respond.

> *"There is a new generation of kids rising up and I prophesy that there is going to be a youth revival. I tell you young Rachel is a martyr. She loved Jesus. The Holy Spirit is getting ready to move in unprecedented ways. There will be a day, Dick, when there are so many young people in this church praying they'll fill the balconies, they'll fill every part of the sanctuary. They will drive from San Francisco, and all over the valley. This city has been targeted by Satan to be one of the next places. Gather the leaders to pray...."*

We heeded to the word of the Lord. Jubilee hosted the *Pray For The Bay* gathering at the San Jose Arena on June 14, 1999 to help counter this death grip on our youth. It was a unity rally for our kids, schools, teachers and police officers. The Arena saw a turnout of nearly 16,000.

Power and unity filled the Arena when enthusiastic local pastors of all denominations throughout the Bay Area assembled for corporate prayer and personal testimonies. Joining this inspiring evening of prayer included a variety of powerful speakers and guests ranging from Grammy award-winner M.C. Hammer to San Francisco 49ers Merton Hanks and Ray Brown. Also present was Grammy award winner Howard Hewitt, and video greetings came from Vice President Al Gore, Lieutenant Governor Cruz Bustamante and San Francisco Mayor Willie Brown. All encouraged the young and old alike in praying and gathering in unity for the Bay Area and the nation after the Columbine tragedy.

Especially touching was heartfelt prayer and testimony from the mother, Beth Nemmo, and sisters of one Columbine victim, Rachel Scott, along with their pastor, Bruce Porter. They encouraged everyone with their Christian testimony declaring that God would use Rachel Scott's tragic death for His glory.

I was introduced to M.C. Hammer for the first time at this particular event. Hammer's dancers had been coming to Jubilee for some time but the connection was never made, until *Pray For The Bay*. We hit it off and began discussing ways to draw the young generation to church. *"Hammer Time"* was born and became a popular night at Jubilee. M.C. Hammer hosted the program that attracted both young and old to come together for worship, deliverance, and healing through Hammer's terrific gospel preaching mixed with invited guests each week and congregational testimonies. Some of his guests included Deezer D from the popular hit television series "ER," Kirk Franklin and Nifty Tom Fifty.

Embracing today's youth is a priority here at Jubilee and in an effort to bridge the gap of communication between the law and our kids, we also hosted "Kids, Cops & Clergy." This became a chance for all parents and their children in the community to come and be a part of this summit with police officers and ministers as panelists. Many concerned parents and youth showed up to this open forum of questions and answers that provided insight and encouragement and most of all prayer.

〜 MOVING THROUGH THE ENEMY'S BLOCKADES

I wanted to take the kingdom of God to San Jose's youth in sort of a large-scale way.

In the mid-1990s we created a nightclub for local youth called *Club J*. Its great atmosphere, music, and camaraderie drew kids away from Satan's turf. Although it was only about two years in the running, we had some good youth turnouts and great wholesome activities and refreshments for the young crowds who came for the fellowship. At one time we even had 2,000 youth show up for a concert. A local radio jock from 97.7 FM set up and broadcast from the Jubilee campus and even promoted Club J! "Big Joe" Lopez was one of them. This was his first introduction to Jubilee. Eventually Big Joe and his best friend Brian became born-again believers as a result.

Years later, Big Joe Lopez was a part of San Francisco's FM 94.9 radio program called the *Dog House*. The Dog House was risqué and pushed the broadcast envelope with dubious language and lewd content. I saw the Dog House therefore as a kind of spiritual blockade set against the minds of our Silicon Valley youth. I wanted to run this blockade.

In 1999 Big Joe invited me as a guest minister to discuss all things spiritual on the Dog House.

Unlike the average churchman or local pastor who would be handicapped with prejudice against the people who hosted a radio program like this – I wasn't, and therefore earned their respect. I moved through this spiritual blockade for two years and had the opportunity to reach hundreds of thousands of Silicon Valley's listening youth on FM 94.9 every morning from 6:00 to 10:00 a.m.

The first year I was a weekly guest, sometimes live in the studio. Other times Big Joe would call me on the phone to query me on controversial spiritual topics. I might be called to bring a counter-argument when, for example, a Muslim guest was brought in, or a person who claims to communicate with the dead, such as nationally known spiritualist Jonathan Edwards.

But Sunday mornings were different: from 8:00 to 9:00 am, M.C. Hammer and I hosted the *God House* on FM 94.9. Often, my son Adam, and Pastor Brian Waller joined Hammer and me with our roundtable exchanges at the radio station. There, we fielded callers' questions about God, the Word of God and other spiritual matters. At times, even Seattle Seahawks' Merton Hanks would also join to encourage and help bring the listeners to the knowledge of Jesus Christ. Unfortunately, after a couple of years another company bought the radio station and the *God House* was cancelled. But thankfully, hundreds of kids visited our church because of it, and many righteous seeds were planted in the hearts of the hearers that will one day germinate. Some plant, some water, but God will give the increase!

In the June of 2000, Dr. Cho invited me to assist him in his crusades and conferences in Zambia, Gabon and Johannesburg, South Africa. I was always willing to join my pastor wherever he wanted me to go, adjusting my schedule accordingly. With my bags in tow, we headed off for the African continent once again. My travels through Africa affected me in a very different way this time. The scenes of millions infected with AIDS everywhere we went astounded me, and certain factions in the government were trying to keep it under wraps. *These people could literally be wiped out in 20 years*, I thought. Forty percent of the entire country is infected with AIDS. God have mercy and visit that country, I pray.

Four months later, I once again joined Dr. Cho in Yokohama, Japan for his Annual Church Growth International Conference. This was the first time I had visited Japan and I was amazed at what I saw. My mind went back to when I was a kid growing up hearing the horrors stories of the Japanese in World War II and how devastated that country became. It was amazing to me that there were no signs of the ravages of war. The Japanese are a very industrious and hard working people and were able to overcome. Riding around downtown Tokyo, the world's largest city, it epitomizes the industrialization that has taken place in Japan. Sleek towering hotels and businesses dot the city's skyline. The picturesque stalls of local vendors were a delight to take in. We also enjoyed a panoramic view of this bustling metropolis from atop Tokyo Tower. Japan had truly recovered and is very prosperous.

Sept. 11, 2001 - The World Changed Forever

On the morning of September 11th I was awakened by a frantic phone call from a friend telling me to turn the television on, it's the end of the world.

I immediately jumped out of bed and grabbed the remote, and as I turned the television on I watched, in shock and disbelief, the New York City skyline's *Twin Towers* literally crumble before my eyes.

I was glued to the television, as millions were that morning trying to understand what was going on. Four hijacked airline passenger jets fully loaded with jet fuel were turned into human cruise missiles by radical Islamists, and they aimed three of them at the *World Trade Center* Twin Towers in New York City and at the *Pentagon* in Washington, D.C.

The mass terror attack produced panic and fear across the nation – America was under attack and no one knew where the terrorists would strike next. The country was shaken and churches across the land were overflowing with people seeking comfort and answers for this unexpected act of war. Jubilee was no different.

For months afterward attendance soared and remained high until things calmed down. Reassuring messages from President George W. Bush promised the American people restoration and accountability for our losses.

Interestingly, the daughter of a couple in our church had been living in New York City and worked across the street from the Twin Towers. Their prodigal daughter was on her way to work that morning and was having difficulty getting there on her usual train route; it had been rerouted several times. While sitting in the train Adriana heard over the loud speaker, "There has been an accident at the World Trade Center. Everyone must evacuate immediately. Don't panic." Adriana got off the train one exit short of the Twin Towers and climbed the stairs from the subway to the street. People were stampeding in her direction away from ground zero in a thick cloud of smoke. She still wasn't sure what was going on. "All I could hear was people crying and sirens going off, non-stop; and, there were no cars in sight. It was sheer chaos and confusion. People were falling and being pushed aside as others ran for their lives," Adriana recalled.

"An eerie feeling came over me," she said.

"I remember my dad telling me about the Rapture... Is this the Rapture?"

When Adriana finally discovered what had happened she was shaken and realized that she had just had a brush with death. She wasn't able to contact her parents because after the first tower was hit it destroyed the satellite communication tower, and as a result all the cell phone lines in the city went dead. She later learned that the train she was originally supposed to ride on was crushed under the rubble of the World Trade Center.

"I felt like God was taking me on a spiritual journey and I honestly felt like I was lost. I lost my sense of direction, and of who I was. I felt like I was walking through darkness."

Her memories of that day were still fresh three years later. "I remember that for the next few months the stench and the odor lingered in the city. Often at night the sea breeze of the Hudson River would carry the smell through the city, a solemn reminder of the lives that were tragically killed that fateful day."

In the weeks and months that followed our church heard many similar testimonies of families that were miraculously spared. I continued to rally our people to pray for the victims and for our national leaders to make the right decisions to guide the destiny of our nation.

FATHERLESS GENERATION

I wasn't raised with a father and I didn't raise my son Adam in his early years, but God is nevertheless redeeming my family. I married my daughter Sarah to Daniel Green in 1999 and they began their family. I now have three grandsons – Nicolas, Michael and Jaden, who call us *Pa* and *Ma*.

My youngest son, Jesse is still in college at the San Francisco Academy of Arts, studying media and the arts, and works for me part-time. Our family is growing and I realize the responsibility of ensuring I leave a legacy for them. Becoming a grandfather has been the best thing for me. Watching my kids grow up and have their own families is a great blessing. My priorities and values of family relationships are maturing as I get older.

One day I was talking with a couple of friends over dinner. I was curious about their upbringing, especially by their fathers.

Mike Hayes told me that his hyper-religious father raised him, and Steve Hage said that he was raised on the streets and that his dad was a druggie. As we continued sharing stories about our childhood, I thought it would be a good idea to have a conference dealing with childhood issues, especially with fathers. I wanted Mike and Steve to come out to Jubilee and share from their experiences so that others could be healed and restored. I also invited other pastors whom I knew would add to the conference, such as, Darroll Hines and Jim Reeves. They agreed, and we convened in February of 2002. My son Adam shared his own experiences, along with my sister Juanita. It was a special time and we saw the Lord do things in those meetings that broke families free from their generational bondages, releasing many from childhood traumas and abuse. True restoration and liberty were no longer imagined or longed for, but were beginning to be realized by many who attended.

JUBILEE'S SPANISH MINISTRY

A well-known Latino couple in our church approached me one afternoon asking me if they could open up a cell group for the Spanish speakers in the community. They were members of Jubilee for years, Mary Lou was in real estate and had assisted our church on some business transactions. But her husband Osbaldo seemed pretty quiet and unassuming.

Osbaldo had gone to Bogotá for three-and-one-half months, spending time with the leaders of ICM and studying the vision. When he returned home from Bogotá in May, he was beginning to feel unsettled and wanted to take the gospel to our Spanish-speaking neighbors. I immediately sent these enthusiastic leaders to Pastor Adam to help direct them, and was not sure how things would work out. Six months after they opened their cell 120 people were attending, and I was truly amazed. Osbaldo and his wife are hard working leaders full of vision and now, after nearly three years, they are pastoring 700 people in the

Spanish services on Sunday mornings.

They are impacting the Spanish communities of *Alviso*, *East Palo Alto* and *Nancy Lane – East San Jose*.

Pastors Osbaldo and Mary Lou Perez have since been to Bogotá many times and are well versed in the vision and what it takes to grow a cell church. They have 3-day *Encounter* weekends every two months, a *School of Leaders, youth services* and *children's ministry,* all geared toward the G-12 vision, only in Spanish. They also interpret for us when Pastor Cesar and Claudia Castellanos come to visit and preach. It gives them opportunity to continue learning from the Castellanos' as they have become like their extended family.

The September 11th testimony I mentioned earlier made reference to a young lady that nearly died in the tragedy. She is the daughter of our Spanish pastors. Shortly after the tragedy, Adriana moved home and a year later she went to Bogotá to study the vision and stayed for three-and-one-half months. She and her sister Melissa assist their parents' in the ministry. It is a family affair and I am pleased with how they are doing. Jubilee's Spanish ministry is fast becoming the largest Spanish speaking church in the Bay Area.

JUBILEE *TRI-VALLEY* DEDICATION

Planning and preparing for special occasions is something I am used to doing. But this particular occasion had significance like no other.

You see I had been grooming my son Adam for the pastorate ever since he gave his life to the Lord. And, now it was time for him to "spread his wings" and take flight to pastor his own church. So Adam forged ahead, uprooted his family, and moved to the rapidly growing suburban community of Livermore, northeast of San Jose. He began having church in storefront buildings and hotels, and was getting used to his new role and surroundings. He was anxious to get a building of his own but waited patiently until Dad was able to come through and assist him. With Dad's help, he was able to lease a building of their own and now it was time to join them to celebrate!

We were excited as Carla and I joined Adam and Michelle at their dedication service on May 18, 2003. As I sat there during the praise and worship it was *déjà vu* recalling my humble beginnings with a start-up church and the journey I've traveled to get to where I am today.

As Adam conveyed the vision to his people, I saw myself in him. I was looking out at all these new leaders in the congregation thinking, *You have a journey ahead of you, son, with challenges and problems waiting for you.* It was indeed one of the highlights of my life and ministry to see my son coming into his own in ministry.

Adam recently secured a lease on a former health spa that is being renovated to facilitate the youth, and a food pantry. He was planning to gut the building but is temporarily using it as a place for the homeless to shower.

God's redemptive plan brought Adam back into my life. Now Adam is doing what his dad does, almost to a tee. Well, what can I say?

MEETING AMERICA'S COMMANDER-IN-CHIEF

Traveling to Washington, D.C. in June of 2003 to meet

President George W. Bush was a highlight for Carla and me. We had met various presidents and dignitaries from other countries so we were acquainted with the protocol and security detail. I was very impressed with his character and personality, having had an opportunity to greet him and have a brief conversation.

"Mr. President, I bring you greetings from the President of Bogotá, Dr. Uribe."

"You know Dr. Uribe?" inquired the President.

"Yes, I do," I kindly replied.

"I also bring you greetings from James Robison. I just had dinner with him the other night."

The President's face lit up, surprised that I knew him, too.

As he was leaving he said, "Give them both my love."

DESTINY HOMES – CARING FOR PEOPLE

Carla and Juanita have been wanting me to open up a women's home for years. In December of 2003 we were debt free and I just wanted to enjoy the fruits of our labors. Well, to appease them I showed up at a home they insisted I inspect. It looked like a Victorian Bed-and-Breakfast Inn and is in downtown San Jose. But I still wasn't interested in buying a home. I had made up my mind that I was only going there to look and not buy.

Driving down First Street on the way back to my office, I was stopped at a red signal light and noticed an older homeless African-American woman dressed in tattered clothing, carrying a shopping cart with a garbage bag of personal belongings. I was hoping the light would quickly turn green so I could flee from the image that was being etched in my mind. It seemed like the light remained red for an eternity. She began walking across the street, and I heard a question – *"Do you really care for these people?"* I was deeply convicted. Driving away from the scene, I had a change of heart, telling the Lord that I would do whatever He wanted me to.

Our church purchased the home. Shortly thereafter another home became available and we purchased it as well.

The testimonies from the women living there are rewarding. From the time the first *Destiny Home* opened there was a waiting list, and now many of those women and children are being cared for through the generosity of Jubilee.

We had an Open House on March 27, 2004. The *700 Club* from Virginia Beach, VA. attended with a camera crew to do a special feature on our Destiny Homes. It later aired on their daily television program – and Jubilee was congratulated as the *"Church of the Week."*

EASTER AT SAN JOSE'S SHARK TANK

On April 11, 2004, Resurrection Sunday, we rented the San Jose Arena – the *Shark Tank* for Easter service, and 16,000 people showed up. Motown legend Smokey Robison, and M.C. Hammer were our special guests and they delivered inspiring messages in song and in the Word of God. City Counsel woman Cindy Chavez was also an invited guest who was there to help raise funds for the homeless kids of the Bay Area. She and I don't agree on many issues, but that didn't stop us from rallying for a good civic cause. The people responded enthusiastically.

"The thing I find so fascinating about him (Dick Bernal) is that he's a spiritual person without being a religious person – religious in the way of being rigid and rule-oriented," Cindy Chavez said. "He doesn't seem to forget that he is human."

Hundreds lined the altar and gave their hearts to the Lord. It never ceases to amaze me how God draws people to these gatherings. We are living in a time when hungry hearts are desperate for God and I am privileged and blessed that God would use me to bring hope to the hurting of the Bay Area.

JUBILEE'S NEW YOUTH FACILITY

Jubilee purchased the future home of our new youth facility in April of 2004. We purchased this 75,000 square foot high-tech building for $13 million dollars and it will be renovated to house our children's and youth ministries. We will provide young people with a wholesome environment so the facility will be equipped with a café, lounge area, pool tables, video games, a computer bar, rock wall climbing, and more. Our youth don't want religion, they are looking for truth and acceptance as they face issues never before seen in past generations. They need our help and I believe that we can positively influence them by providing an environment to build important relationships through social interaction, discipleship, and having church.

The youth ministry has also implemented the G-12 vision with their own three-day Encounters. The youth run cells that are networked throughout the Bay Area. A School of Leaders will begin, as well as many other avenues for training and building leaders within their own ministry. Young people aren't our future they are our present!

JUBILEE-*MORGAN HILL* DEDICATION

Morgan Hill is a small town some 10 miles south of San Jose. It is a town where Carla and I lived for 13 years, and a town I love. Planting a Jubilee campus in Morgan Hill was exciting for me because Jubilee is now fulfilling its call to spread the gospel beyond our home in San Jose.

I had my eye on our Singles pastors whom I knew would be suited for the job. They had been involved in other leadership roles at the time as well. I began dialoguing with Pastor Carlos and Maxine Alfarez for a year or so, planting seeds about pastoring in the South Bay. After awhile their hearts began to shift and their desire to pastor in this thriving community became evident.

On May 23rd the dedication service went off as planned. The place was packed and the people embraced Carlos and Maxine. Observing them leave the comfortable nest of Jubilee-San Jose is something I have enjoyed. They face challenges like any other pastor would, but I believe in them and I know they can make a go of it. They are close to home and I continue to encourage and instruct them on the qualities of pastoring.

CHAPTER 12

A GUIDING INFLUENCE IN MY LIFE

So what if you fall? It is one thing to pick yourself up after a fall, and another thing to discover what caused your fall. If you profit from your mistakes as I have, something is guiding your life. Today as never before I seek wisdom like silver and I search for it like hidden treasure.

I'll be the first to say that life can be a discouraging mentor, but *Woe* if we neglect wisdom. As I've advanced in life I'm fortunate to have it as my guide to life.

By nature I am a non-confrontational person, but I have learned that without confrontation you will be run over. I am learning to speak the truth in love and be strong when I know something's right.

At times, I have hired staff who came highly qualified and gifted but the chemistry wasn't right. Trusting people is a necessary part of working with a staff. Honestly, you don't know until they work for you whether they are right for the position or not. That is the necessary weeding-out process and you can't be afraid to trust. You must know that you will hire some wrong people that will cause problems, but that doesn't mean you need to micro-manage your ministry. I am listening to my wife's counsel and discernment on these matters much more today than in earlier years.

Do I have any regrets? No. I am a better person today for

the experiences I've had, good and bad. I have had leaders in the church take flocks of people with them when they left Jubilee. This hurts any pastor, but I am always comforted by the words of a friend that I've never forgotten:

> *"Is it a debt owed or a seed sowed? If you are going to hold something against someone as though they owe you something then God can't bless you. If you look at it as a seed sown, then a seed has life, 30,60,100-fold."*

I now find myself also drawn toward building strong personal relationships with my pastors on staff. Being in the G-12 vision it fosters relationship building, especially with those who are in your circle of 12. We spend quality time enjoying each other's company. Ministry is hard work, so it is good to take the time to simply unwind.

THE ELOQUENCE OF *RHEMA*

If I can imagine the God of the Universe revealing His will to *Dick Bernal* during times of need, how might He do it?

God plants Himself in the conscience of man. If God were to speak through a man – wouldn't that be His most eloquent word?

Over the years I've been amazed at how a *rhema,* a word from God, can change one's life.

My earliest rhema from heaven was soon after graduating from Bible school as a young Christian. My sister Juanita asked me, "Why don't you start a church, Dick? We like the way you teach."

Although I was repelled by the idea, a voice from the depths of my being whispered, *"Listen to your sister. She is speaking for Me. It is My will for you to pastor right here, son."*

As Providence would have it, I obeyed God's mandate.

More recently, my rhema from God was told to me by my visit to Bogotá when I witnessed thousands of zealous Colombian youth reverencing and worshiping God. With that, I had a reformed outlook at youth. I bolted home determined to speed up the G-12 cell system in our church. God had indeed spoken to me through Colombia's youth.

Another example came from a friend, Rich Marshall who helped co-host a revival with me at our church a couple of years ago. One little phrase I declared during the service resulted in a huge change in his life. I stepped to the pulpit and gave a simple greeting, *"Good evening kings, good evening priests!"*

Rich was perplexed by my announcement, but curious. He wondered what I meant. After the service he came to the back room and queried me. I explained that the idea is found in Revelation 1:6, where God has made us "kings and priests unto Himself." Later I gave him my two teaching tapes on Kings and Priests —Rich was *euphoric!* He proceeded to preach for about 12 Sundays on this subject, and later wrote a book about God in the marketplace. Everywhere I go people have Rich Marshall's book, *God @ Work.*

Today Rich Marshall takes his marketplace message of God's kings and priests all over the world – all the result of a simple *rhema* word in church.

Interestingly, my worship leader for many years, Ron Kenoly, drew inspiration for writing Jubilee worship songs based upon *"Pastor Dick's sermons,"* as he put it. Yes, maybe just a word, or a phrase in my sermon would be a *rhema* to fire Ron's imagination. A third of Ron's songs were inspired in this very way.

A simple word fitly spoken comes from God and it can inspire enormous change in a man's life for the better!

MY DEBT OF GRATITUDE

I can therefore confidently testify that most of the wisdom imparted to me has been through other people. This is a kingdom principle and is, to me, God's most persuasive speech.

What I like about the Lord is that whether we're quick studies or slow, whether we grew up as saints from the crib or played craps for most of our lives, when we enter the kingdom of God, we become His children. And, when we commit to grow together in our families, with friends, and as members of our churches, something wonderful happens. We all continue learning about God from one another.

There were times that my marriage and ministry suffered so much stress that I didn't think I could survive. The only thing I could think of were people who loved us and were praying for us. Sometimes I've put my wife through so much that I've wondered why she didn't trade me in on a new model. But Carla can forgive anyone for anything, and she does this for me.

I've learned from Carla, although it drives me crazy at times, that you can pray in the Spirit even in dreadful moments. Time and again I've seen her do this. She finds the joy of victory in her heart even before the answer comes. Now, that's faith!

Others whom I owe a debt of gratitude:

Pastor Cho, who is pastor of the world's largest church, has taught me that you can doubt yourself and wonder about your calling and still pastor a mega-church. Dr. Cho is the most transparent minister that I've ever known; he has a rare and uncanny ability to share his weaknesses and be cheered by his congregation for his honesty. I hope that I am learning to do the same. Traveling extensively with him over the years, he has also taught me how to be a statesman, and I indeed have learned from the very best.

I admire Jack Hayford, pastor of the *Church on the Way*, because he shows that you can be intelligent and still be a Pentecostal. Jack is so educated that I need to take a dictionary to his meetings just so I can say, "Amen." In the past, too often dear souls who had Pentecostal fire put down higher education. We have much to learn from each other.

Robert Schuller of *Crystal Cathedral* told me to be myself no matter how much pressure there is to conform to my peers. Robert Schuller took a lot of flack for his positive thinking approach, but he was simply putting the Gospel in positive terms. Millions are blessed because he stuck with it.

From that precious saint of God, Oral Roberts, I've learned how to be strong as horseradish and yet have people still love me. Oral is the strongest man I've ever been around, yet he is as sweet as a rose. He'll tell you the truth even if he knows you won't like it. He needed that strength of character to confront all the powerful diseases he came against over the years. "Dick, never be ashamed of the message of faith and healing. Stay the course." In my book, Oral Roberts is a man's man.

Lester Sumrall taught me that a man with a vision doesn't

have time to die until he's finished his course. At the age of 83 years, Dr. Sumrall finished his course and went on to be with the Lord. Both Lester Sumrall and T.L. Osborne instilled in me a world-view and a heart for God's mission frontier.

Mike Hayes, Jack Deere and Larry Stockstill, my relationship with these men has become like iron sharpening iron. I never leave them without pondering or reflecting on something profound.

LAST WORDS

Now that I am 60, I am believing God for an Abrahamic anointing. Like Abraham I'm blessed with children and grandchildren, and Abraham began his ministry at 60. Abraham is a man I want to study – his life and journey with God.

Leaving a legacy for my children and my children's children is what I will continue to do for the rest of my days. I want to be sure that my children continue to press on in faith, and abide in the vision that is burning in me.

And, Dick Bernal —what do I have to teach anyone? Maybe that you can get knocked down without being knocked out. My eternal optimism reveals to me that you can always get up and try again – the glass is half full rather than half empty.

I have always acknowledged that I have made enough mistakes in my life to sink a ship. My life is an open book. But somehow even in the midst of my weaknesses and failures God has been able to use me. I have been greatly misunderstood and judged by my peers and have made a few enemies along the way. But, I suppose it comes with the territory of refusing to be a traditional pastor, minister, or religious fanatic. I've never been afraid to cross lines to reach those who may never go to church. The church isn't confined within the four walls of a structure. The apostle Paul said it so clearly, "Be all things to all people that you might win some." I am a peculiar preacher who often goes where others fear to tread. Perhaps my life story is unique and maybe it's because I serve a God who made me that way.

Being in my line of spiritual work I would never have imagined that I would meet and interact with some of the most powerful and influential people in the world. When Jesus declared, "You are the salt of the earth," this defined the parameters of my gospel witness. I was to cut across denominational, racial, and cultural lines to reach and influence people for God

I have come to realize that many of the people the Lord sent my way were just people with problems. No matter how famous or how rich, they needed help. Everyone needs God in their lives, and God uses Carla and me to minister to them, sometimes in the most peculiar ways.

Who could have imagined that God would use this ole' iron-worker-turned-ambassador for Christ the way He has? But life and its end are God's prerogatives. My personal history is simply the operation of God's grace. I am an extremely blessed man and I give all the glory to my Lord and Savior Jesus Christ.

Finally, being placed in a position of leadership and influence should be the story of *every* Christian. The church I pastor in San Jose, California has grown since 1980 from just Carla and me and several family members to over 12,000 members, a real sign, I believe, of God's blessing.

No, my father really didn't own a gas station – my FATHER owns it all!